Brecht: a study

Brecht: a study

by

MICHAEL MORLEY

Senior Lecturer in Drama
The Flinders University of South Australia

HEINEMANN
LONDON
ROWMAN AND LITTLEFIELD
TOTOWA, NEW JERSEY

832.912
Mo

ISBN (Heinemann) 0 435 38594 1
ISBN (Rowman and Littlefield) 0–87471–935–6

Library of Congress Cataloging in Publication Data

Morley, Michael.
  Brecht: a study.

  Bibliography: p.
  1. Brecht, Bertolt, 1898–1956—Criticism and
interpretation.
PT2603. R397Z773   832′.9′12   76–50004
ISBN 0–87471–935–6

Published by
Heinemann Educational Books Ltd
48 Charles Street, London W1X 8AH
This edition published in the United States 1977
by Rowman and Littlefield, Totowa, New Jersey
Printed in Great Britain by
Richard Clay (The Chaucer Press) Ltd
Bungay, Suffolk

Contents

Acknowledgements

The author of any study of Brecht cannot ignore the ground-work of all those who have preceded his attempt 'to better the instruction'. While I hope that this guide makes a modest contribution in this direction, I do not claim that it can supplant the invaluable studies of, above all, Reinhold Grimm and John Willett. This study owes much to their approach to Brecht criticism and especially to the latter's personal encouragement and assistance over the years. Any flaws or inconsistencies in the interpretations advanced here are in no way attributable to his generously proffered corrective guidelines.

I should also like to express my thanks to the staff of the Brecht Archive, especially to Herta Ramthun for her unstinting helpfulness during my time there. Professor G. P. Butler kindly interrupted a holiday to read the manuscript and make a number of improvements. Mrs S. Yates and Mrs S. Fraser typed the manuscript: to the latter, in particular, thanks are due for completing the final draft at such short notice.

Finally, I am grateful to my wife Pamela both for her good-humoured patience and her refusal to take either the author or the subject of this study too seriously. If too much of the *tierischer Ernst* Brecht so abhorred remains, the fault is certainly neither his, nor hers.

M. M.

The author and publishers wish to thank Suhrkamp Verlag for permission to quote extracts from the *Gesammelte Werke*, from *Arbeitsjournal 1938–55*, from *Über Lyrik*, and from *Schriften zum Theater*, by Bertolt Brecht. The English translations of these extracts, given in the footnotes, are by Michael Morley.

1

Literary Biography

Eugen Berthold Brecht was born on 10 February 1898, in Augsburg, Bavaria. His father was a clerk in the local paper-mill, who later rose to the position of manager of the firm. Much has been written on his relationship with his family and his bourgeois background: much, if not all of it, is speculative, owing more to preconceived psychological notions of social estrangement and/or father-hatred than to the facts. It is clear from his poetry and the evidence of his friends that the young Brecht was deeply attached to his mother; but it is wrong to imagine that this indicated a dislike for, and rejection of his father. Although the latter was not in favour of Brecht's becoming a writer, he never at any stage actively prevented him: on the contrary—he was even prepared to allow the young Brecht to make use of the firm's secretaries to type out his first play *Baal*. Brecht himself is partly responsible for the currency of rumours about his early estrangement from the family. But his own later pronouncements on his upbringing and surroundings should not be cited as proof positive that from the outset he was at odds with his environment and the social milieu to which he belonged. For in such matters Brecht is notoriously unreliable. Take for instance the following account he gave to Sergei Tretyakov of his experiences as a 'medical orderly' in the 'military hospital' in Augsburg (an experience which, it is frequently stated, was the direct source of his pacifist and anti-militaristic views):

> . . . If the doctor ordered me: 'Amputate a leg, Brecht', I would answer: 'Yes, your excellency', and cut off the leg. If I was told: 'Make a trepanning', I opened the man's skull and tinkered with his brains.

The exaggeration and macabre irony of Brecht's description should both be obvious enough to warn the reader that the facts should be regarded with some scepticism. But critics have disregarded the tone of Brecht's account, lifted the apparently factual statements out of context and come up with assertions about his time in the *Reservelazarett* (reserve hospital) which are as unsound in their facts as they are exotic in their fiction. There is ample evidence to hand, in the form of Schmidt's study, to provide the corrective to such flights of fancy. And, unfortunately, this type of problem is not an isolated one in the case of Brecht. In many cases he was partly or wholly responsible for the evolution of a personal mythology. He wrote, for instance, to Herbert Ihering that at university he studied medicine and learnt how to play the guitar—a paradoxical observation whose obvious irony has too often been disregarded. He did, in fact, enrol as a student of medicine—but to please his mother and escape the draft. And although his time at University may indeed have improved his technique, he had been playing the guitar while still at school. Furthermore, it is clear from the evidence of friends and of Brecht himself that, for a time, he also attended lectures on German language, literature and philosophy—notably, those given by the *Theaterprofessor* and critic Artur Kutscher, the friend and biographer of Frank Wedekind. Kutscher's lectures and seminars were popular with the students, not only because of his ability as a lecturer, but because he was at the time the only professor who was holding courses on contemporary literature. But Brecht's interest even in these soon waned, and by November 1921 his commitment to University studies had become so desultory that his name was removed from the books.

The 'orderly in a military hospital' tale can likewise be shown to be largely fictitious: in fact, he was a *Sanitätshelfer* (orderly) in the sick-bay set aside for soldiers suffering from venereal disease. He does not appear to have taken his responsibilities particularly seriously. He took advantage of his superior's relaxed attitude, turned up for his duties dressed to the nines and carrying a cane, and on one occasion even went so far as to have the family maid deliver the evening sick-call list to the medical officer!

But to return to the facts of his biography. Brecht's mother was Lutheran, his father Catholic: he was baptized in the *Barfüsserkirche*, but throughout his early years retained an interest in Catholic liturgy and ritual. His school years saw the emergence of at least two traits which were to become characteristic both of his work and personality: the forming of a wide circle of intimate friends and collaborators (among them Caspar Neher, who was later to win fame as a distinguished stage-designer, Georg Geyer, Georg Pfanzelt and Otto Müllereisert, stylized portraits of whom are to be found in a number of early poems), and the interest in the Bible, biblical phraseology, and poetic forms such as the psalm, hymn and chorale.

The literary and cultural climate in Germany at the time was largely conditioned by the works and philosophy of the Expressionists. In poetry, drama, fiction and the plastic arts the emphasis was on the primacy of the artist's vision, rather than on the need to register reality in a precise or recognizable form. Consequently much Expressionist art and literature is notabel for its use of distortion and for an at times excessive emphasis on the grotesque. Yet equally important—at least to writers like Georg Kaiser and Franz Werfel—was the intensely subjective belief in the possibility of the spiritual regeneration of man. The young Brecht was certainly familiar with Expressionist poetry and prose: and traces of the Expressionist style and vision can be discerned in his earliest literary efforts, though these were relatively undistinguished. 'Der brennende Baum' (The Burning Tree) (*GW8*, p. 3) and the one-act play *Die Bibel* (The Bible) are largely of historical interest, though the latter foreshadows thematic elements to be found in some of the later works. During the years 1914–15 he wrote a number of poems concerned with the war (among them, a poem in praise of the Kaiser)—most of which give little hint of the anti-militaristic attitude he was later to adopt. The year 1916 sign-posts a significant change in Brecht's outlook and in his poetry: first there came his caustic and critical examination of Horace's

motto 'Dulce est et decorum pro patria mori', and, a month
later, the appearance of the poem 'Das Lied von der Eisenbahntruppe von Fort Donald' (The Song of the Railroad Gang
from Fort Donald) (*GW8*, pp. 13–14) published under the name
'Bert Brecht'. This poem deals, in a slightly over-stated and
clumsy fashion, with a theme which is to become the hallmark
of much of his early poetry and drama—the conflict between
man and nature. The men of the railway gang are the literary
godfathers to all the subsequent outlaw-figures of the early
work. Having now found a congenial theme, it was time for
him to seek out the appropriate forms; and for these Brecht
turned to the traditional *Lied* and ballad—a daring step at a
time when Benn, Werfel, Stramm and Becher were being seen
as the inventors of a new poetic language which held out excit-
ing prospects for the development of German poetry. The choice
of these traditional forms was already a clear indication of
Brecht's refusal to follow a 'literary' tradition—a tradition in
which Literature was both spelt with, and discussed in, capital
letters. Brecht chose an 'unliterary', or—in Hans Mayer's
words—'plebeian tradition': plebeian in the sense that he went
back to those forms associated with *Volksdichtung* (folk poetry)
and popular tradition. Those qualities which typified both the
strengths and weaknesses of Expressionist verse—the formless-
ness, hyperbole and breaking down of the structure of language,
together with the nihilism and frequent hysteria—found little
response in the young Brecht. He turned to the traditional
forms, because of, rather than in spite of, their regularity and
the control they demanded: they represented structures within
which he could develop his own essentially anarchic yet positive
view of life, and the themes which reflected this.

The apotheosis of this early attitude comes in his first drama
Baal, a work which gives clear evidence of the young Brecht's
gift for exuberant and vigorous writing. It is very much the
product of his years in Augsburg, and the life he led there. As
the first full-scale work of a twenty-year-old author, it is an
astonishing work, and a far more individual one than his second
play *Trommeln in der Nacht* (Drums in the Night), whose setting
is a rather indistinct Berlin. This drama, which mixes tragi-

comedy and satire, purports—without much success—to be about the 'Spartakus' uprising. For the revolutionary background, Brecht made use of the collapse of the Bavarian Soulet Republic which he had observed in Augsburg and Munich. When he left Augsburg to enrol at the University in 1917, he had also to find rooms in Munich, and during the next few years, he moved constantly between the two cities. The experience of Munich meant a widening of his horizons, and brought him into contact with writers and critics, who, in Augsburg, had been mere names. The move to Munich did not (at least at this stage) signify a complete break with Augsburg and any imagined 'provincial' aspects of the life there. Throughout his life, Brecht's links with the city of his childhood and adolescence remained strong: inevitably, he came to view some aspects of the life there in a somewhat critical light, but he never at any stage rejected that background which had had such a formative influence on him and his work—the river Lech, the *Plärrer* (the Augsburg fair), the nightly serenades, the circle of friends, the memories of childhood and adolescence. In spite of all the differences in temperament, Brecht's experience of Augsburg is as crucial to an understanding of his early work as Joyce's experience of Dublin and Lawrence's experience of the villages round Nottingham are to theirs. Critics have commented on the distinctive character of Brecht's links with Southern Germany and with the city of his youth: but perhaps the most concise summing up of the mark it left on Brecht is provided by Max Frisch in his *Tagebuch 1966-71*:

> Ein Augsburger mit Berlin als Arbeitsplatz, ein Sprachgebundener, Herkunft nicht als Wappen, aber als unvertauschbare Bedingtheit: die selbstverständliche Anerkennung dieser Bedingtheit.[1] (p. 25)

Memories of Augsburg and the life there are to be found in the poetry from the years in exile and also in some of the last

---

[1] 'A native of Augsburg with Berlin as his place of work, a man tied to his language, his origins not as a coat of arms but as an irreplaceable conditionality: The natural recognition of this conditionality.'

poems; and there is an as yet unpublished prose extract from the last years in which Brecht describes, with notable lack of sentimentality and preciousness, the childhood games with tin soldiers in which he and his friends became keenly involved. So much so that on the occasion of his troops being defeated, Brecht resorted to more direct physical measures to rectify matters!

Nevertheless, Augsburg was too small for Brecht's plans; and Munich was not the intellectual or cultural centre of Germany he was looking for. He needed a larger, more public stage. And for this he had to go to Berlin, the metropolis, with its mixture of life-styles imported from the Anglo-Saxon world, Europe and the rest of Germany. Once there he thought he would find both the audience and the new directions for his work he was hoping for. He arrived in Berlin in 1920; enthused over its fascination and the rhythm of life there, but returned, unsuccessful and somewhat disillusioned, to Munich and Augsburg. At this time, in addition to his poetry and a number of dramatic projects he was writing regular drama criticism for the *Volkswille*, a left-wing newspaper. Already in these early articles can be found his impatience with reactionary trends in the drama and with production techniques of the time.

By 1921, the financial and artistic success he was seeking was still proving elusive. He became interested in the possibility of working for the cinema and, with Neher, wrote a film-script *Drei im Turm* (Three Men in a Tower). Later in the year his short story 'Bargan lässt es sein' ('Bargan lets things be') was published in the *Neuer Merkur*. It is a strange tale of pirates and the homosexual attraction between Bargan and one of his band which leads ultimately to his downfall: but it was the first work of Brecht's to reach a wide audience, and, no doubt emboldened by this success, he decided to make a second visit to Berlin in an attempt to establish himself there. But again his efforts were to meet with failure, and he was admitted to the 'Charité' suffering from 'malnutrition'. (This was according to his own version: in fact he was suffering from pyelo-nephritis, a far less romantic disease than malnutrition!) The time in

Berlin did, however, prove fruitful in at least one respect; he met Arnolt Bronnen and the two struck up a firm friendship which led to their being identified as the two *enfants terribles* of German literature. But notoriety is not always synonymous with success. Brecht was known, but he was far from winning the acclaim he sought, and once again he returned to Munich. It was in September 1922 that the first sign of a breakthrough came, with the production of *Trommeln in der Nacht*, which was followed by the award of the prestigious Kleist-Prize for his first three plays.

In spite of further success in Munich in the following year, Brecht was still convinced of the need for a move. He had met Helene Weigel in 1923, and there seems little doubt that her presence in Berlin had a part to play in his final decision to move there. So it was that in 1924 Brecht finally settled in Berlin, where he was to stay until he fled Germany in 1933. It was to be the scene of some remarkable triumphs and *succès de scandale*. In much the same way that Augsburg and Munich provided him with contacts, friends and collaborators, Berlin was to prove similarly productive. The period in Berlin saw the beginnings of friendships and collaborations which were to last for many years—with the actors Alexander Granach, Peter Lorre, Oscar Homolka and Ernst Busch; with the writers and critics Karl Korsch, Walter Benjamin and Fritz Sternberg; with the composers Kurt Weill and Hanns Eisler; with the directors and stage-writers Erwin Piscator, Slatan Dudow and Emil Burri. It was here too that he met Elisabeth Hauptmann, who was to become his secretary and life-long literary adviser and editor.

By the late twenties he had, as a convinced Marxist, become more involved in the literary and political scene. His concern for the political and social problems of the time and his outspokenness and championing of the Communist cause soon had him in trouble with the authorities. He had been a marked man for some time because of his left-wing attitudes and writings; and the disruption of performances of his plays by Nazi sympathizers and the banning and mutilation of the film *Kuhle Wampe* by the official censors were clear signs of

how dangerous the Nazis considered him. On the day following the Reichstag fire he fled from Germany, to spend the
next fourteen years in exile.

These years were to prove years of hardship and privation
for Brecht and his family—though the self-pity and laments for
lost status and identity that one finds in the writings of a number of German émigrés (notably Stefan Zweig, Karl Wolfskehl
and even Alfred Döblin) are conspicuously absent from his
work. It is, admittedly, understandable that writers like Zweig
should feel keenly the loss of their fame, their audience and
the freedom to publish their works—but in every respect, he
was in a far more comfortable position than Brecht. And, in the
light of his personal and social status, it is difficult to feel much
sympathy with many of his complaints about a plight which
was a cause for envy rather than mortification. Brecht on the
other hand, though he did not have as difficult a time as, for
instance, Dessau or Benjamin, nevertheless was dependent for
most of the time on the generosity of friends and the handouts
—in the shape of any work that was available—of film- or
play-producers. But, instead of any lament or loud complaints
about personal grievances being voiced in the poetry of these
years, we find Brecht describing his situation in lines which have
become a dispassionate motto for his years in exile:

> Gingen wir doch, öfter als die Schuhe die Länder wech-
> selnd.[1]   (*GW 9*, p. 725)

The image achieves its effect both by virtue of its everyday
associations and the laconic, matter-of-fact tone. Taken in
conjunction with the following lines from the cycle '1940', it
affords an illustration as epigrammatic as it is revealing of
Brecht's distinctive treatment of the theme of exile which is
at once convincing and moving in its restraint:

1940 VIII

Auf der Flucht vor meinen Landsleuten
Bin ich nun nach Finnland gelangt. Freunde
Die ich gestern nicht kannte, stellten ein paar Betten

[1] For we went, changing countries more often than shoes.

In saubere Zimmer. Im Lautsprecher
Höre ich die Siegesmeldungen des Abschaums. Neu-
    gierig
Betrachte ich die Karte des Erdteils. Hoch oben in
    Lappland
Nach dem Nördlichen Eismeer zu
Sehe ich noch eine kleine Tür.[1]   (*GW 9*, p. 819)

Yet it was a time of difficulty and also pain; there were problems with the Danish authorities, and difficulties in obtaining
visas first for Sweden, and then for the U.S.A. Brecht had to
promise not to become involved in any political activity in
Sweden, and was forced to use the pseudonym John Kent for
some of his writings—none of which, of course, were published
at the time. As it became increasingly clear that the Nazi
armies might overrun Scandinavia, Brecht was forced to decide to flee Europe. Significantly, he chose not Russia as a
refuge (where so many German Marxists and Communists,
among them personal friends, had vanished) but the U.S.A.
He had, in fact, wanted to leave Finland in August 1940,
but it was not until May 1941 that the visas for both his family
and his collaborators, Margarete Steffin and Ruth Berlau,
came through. They left Helsinki for Leningrad, Moscow and
Vladivostock on 15 May. It was on the train trip from Moscow
to Vladivostock, on 4 June, that news reached him of the death
of Margarete Steffin, who, seriously ill from tuberculosis, had
stayed behind in Moscow. It was probably the greatest loss
Brecht was to suffer. Her death left a gap which could not be
filled. Subsequent poems and diary entries show how conscious
he remained of his dependence on her, and how deeply he mis-
sed her, both on a personal level and for his work.

The years in America were as difficult as anything he had

---

[1] On my flight from my countrymen
I have now reached Finland. Friends
Who yesterday were unknown to me, set up a few beds
In clean rooms. Over the radio
I hear the victory bulletins of the scum of the earth. Inquisitively
I study the map of the continent. High up in Lapland
Towards the Northern Arctic
I can still see a small door.

faced previously: the commercialization of art and the control exercised by the film magnates, together with the capitalistic and monopolistic system within which everyone was forced to work—all these aspects of life in Hollywood left Brecht depressed and frustrated. But for the help of friends in the film industry and his own never-failing resilience, he would surely have gone under, or, at the least, lost both the urge and the ability to write. The time in California was not, it is true, as productive as the years 1933-41—years which saw the writing of the dramas and poems which are the peak of his mature work. But the poetry written in America cannot be dismissed lightly, nor his collaboration with Charles Laughton on *Leben des Galilei* (Galileo), nor, indeed, dramas such as *Die Gesichte der Simone Machard* (The Visions of Simone Machard) or *Der kaukasische Kreidekreis* (The Caucasian Chalk Circle). Nevertheless, one point needs to be made clear: Brecht's involvement with the film industry, and the need to work on film-scripts as the surest way of earning enough money to live, undoubtedly contributed to the falling-off in volume of his work during these years. He had numerous projects in mind, but most remained unrealized, or, at best, only partly realized. The complicated account of his ventures in the film world is of considerable importance to an understanding of his position at the time, and it is clear that James K. Lyon's study of this period—an extract of which has already appeared—will fill a large gap in Brecht studies.

But Brecht's links with Hollywood were to bring him to the attention of the public in a way in which he had not expected. In 1947, the 'Red scare' was coming into its own, at the instigation of Senator McCarthy and with the unfailing support of that inquisitorial body masquerading under the name of the 'Committee on Unamerican Activities'. Brecht, along with a number of other writers and actors—among them John Garfield, Larry Parks, the Eisler brothers and Dalton Trumbo—was summoned to appear before the Committee. It was investigating the infiltration of the film industry by left-wingers and Marxists, and Brecht was suspect because of his connections. The hearing was a farce: unlike some of the others who appeared, Brecht did not invoke the Fifth Amendment, but chose to answer all the questions put to him. The transcript of the trial, together with the tape of the proceedings, is one of the best illustrations of his theatrical abilities. As in the trial scenes from his own dramas, the accused ends up virtually running the proceedings: Brecht used to devastating effect the practised naïveté which Schweyk calls on in all his dealings with those in authority. At the same time, the farcical nature of the proceedings in this particular case should not make one forget that Brecht was considerably luckier than many others. A truer and fuller account of what these proceedings entailed for less fortunate witnesses is given in Eric Bentley's sobering *Thirty Years of Treason*. After the hearing, Brecht could afford to remark jokingly to an acquaintance that it was better than being tried by the Nazis—they wouldn't have let him smoke. But he seems to have been somewhat blind to the fate of some of his fellows, though he had by this time returned to Europe, and hence was not affected in the same way by the events in America.

The last years were marked by his emergence as one of the most important figures in European drama, and by the revolutionary impact of his methods of production on a wide range of directors. He was increasingly subject to the pressures of work and demands on his time; so much so that he had little opportunity to continue with his own writing. With the exception of the adaptation of *Coriolanus* and the unrevised *Turandot* he wrote nothing for the stage which could compare with the achievements of the thirties and forties. For most of the time he was fully occupied with the staging of his own works and of stage adaptations of the dramas of writers as dissimilar as Synge and Strittmater, Hauptmann and Molière, Lenz and Kleist. Under his guidance and with his wife as artistic director, the Berliner Ensemble established itself as the most important and distinctive theatre company in Europe. With the facilities at his disposal and the massive subsidies made available to him by the East German government, Brecht could afford to spend weeks, even months, in rehearsing a play: and the opportunity of working with him and studying his methods of production attracted directors, actors, musicians and stage-designers from all over Germany.

But if the last years were a time of comfort and fame, they were not free from controversy, both in the East and West. The '*Lukullus*-affair' caused a row with the authorities in East Berlin, while the *Herrnburger Bericht* (Report from Herrn-burg) (mercifully omitted from the *Gesammelte Werke*), was the cause of an even bigger commotion in the West. But both were surpassed by the storm of controversy which surrounded Brecht's reaction to the events of 16 and 17 June 1953. A few points should be noted which have some bearing on any final assessment of his attitude to the uprising in Berlin. Perhaps the most helpful analysis of the problematical situation in which Brecht found himself is given by Thomas Brown in a short but carefully argued article. In it he dispels a number of all too easily formed preconceptions about Brecht and his re-actions.

It is, first of all, unfair to accuse him of cynicism for, on the one hand, refusing to condemn Ulbricht in public, and, on the other, setting down his sharp and satirical criticism in poems which were only to appear some years later. His own position was, at the time, still not completely secure against attack—or so he felt. But more important than this was his conviction that the uprising itself was being exploited by *agents provoca-teurs* in and from the West and this could well lead to a re-surgence of Fascism. To anyone judging the events from the outside, this may seem like the sophistry which the Russians advanced in support of their intervention in Czechoslovakia. But the situations are not similar. There was free and uncon-trolled access between East and West Berlin, and, at the time of the uprising, nationalist forces were intent on exploiting any possible advantage which might be gained from the disarray. Brecht's own remarks on this point, both at the time and subsequently, are clear evidence of his feelings on the matter: and it is not surprising that, involved as he was with the events of 1929–33, he would not quickly have forgotten those aspects of the present uprising which recalled the past. This is not the same as saying that the disturbances in the

Berlin of the late twenties and early thirties were similar to those that took place in Berlin in 1953. But Brecht thought he detected an undercurrent of feeling which reminded him all too uncomfortably of what he had seen twenty years earlier. In a letter to Peter Suhrkamp he wrote that he had seen not only demonstrating workers but also:

> . . . allerlei deklassierte Jugendliche, die durch das Brandenburger Tor, über den Potsdamer Platz, auf der Warschauer Brücke, kolonnenweise eingeschleust waren . . .[1]

And he went on to say that he had been struck by the sharp, brutal figures from the Nazi era,

> . . . die man seit Jahren nicht mehr in Haufen hatte auftreten sehen, und die doch immer da gewesen waren.[2]

Yet another note to a friend confirms this reaction. To Erwin Leiser he wrote:

> Die Sozialistische Einheitspartei hat Fehler begangen, die für eine sozialistische Partei sehr schwerwiegend sind und Arbeiter gegen sie aufbrachten. Ich gehöre ihr nicht an. Aber ich respektiere viele ihrer historischen Errungen-schaften, und ich fühlte mich ihr verbunden, als sie— nicht ihrer Fehler, sondern ihrer Vorzüge wegen—von faschistischem und kriegstreiberischem Gesindel ange-griffen wurde. Im Kampf gegen Krieg und Faschismus stand und stehe ich an ihrer Seite.[3]

One might object that his comments are couched in language suspiciously close to the jargon of the party ideologues; but

[1] . . . all kinds of 'declassed' youths, who had flooded in files through the Brandenburg Gate, over Potsdamer Platz, across the Warschauer Brücke . . .

[2] . . . which for years one hadn't seen appear in large numbers, yet which had always been there.

[3] The Socialist Unity Party has made mistakes which are of grave con-sequence for a socialist party and which aroused workers against it. I do not belong to the party. But I do respect many of its historic achievements, and I felt myself allied with it when it was attacked by a fascist and warmongering mob—not on account of its mistakes but on account of its merits. In the struggle against war and Fascism I stood and stand by its side.

when one takes these in conjunction with his criticisms of the party's mistakes, it seems that, rightly or wrongly, he did have genuine reservations at the time. It was these reservations which led to his own failure to ally himself expressly and in public with the workers: and it was these reservations which were to trouble him for some time afterwards, so much so that in several of the *Buckower Elegien* (Buckow Elegies) his candour and self-criticism reveal clearly a sense of personal failure in the face of events.

There is little doubt that the strenuous demands of his position as 'artistic adviser' (which entailed engaging actors, musicians and directors, and deciding on the repertoire for the company) left him mentally and physically exhausted. The last two years in Berlin were marred by ill-health; as early as 1952 he had for various reasons contemplated going into what he termed 'chinesisches Exil',[1] and in 1955 he was taking steps to acquire a house in Denmark to which he could retire when he needed to. The house in Buckow was a refuge for him while he was in Berlin; but if he wished to write, it frequently meant rising early in the morning and working through till breakfast. Thus it was that he turned more and more to his poetry. The cycle of *Buckower Elegien* stands out as a work which can take its place beside the great cycles of the thirties; in addition, there are a number of short personal poems which lose nothing in comparison with the best of the poems from the early and middle periods. Such poems are notable for their precise balance between observation and reflection, and for the controlled language which allows Brecht to present himself in a series of candid self-portraits in which he never assumes a pose of ingratiating self-revelation. There is no better example of these qualities, nor indeed a more fitting epitaph to the last years than the following poem, written shortly before his death:

> Als ich in weissem Krankenzimmer der Charité
> Aufwachte gegen Morgen zu

[1] This term, explained by Brecht in his 'Geburtstagsbrief an Karin Michaelis' of 1942 (*GW 19*, pp. 477–8) does not mean 'exile in China'. As he points out in the letter: 'The Chinese poets and philosophers would go into exile like ours go into academies.'

Und die Amsel hörte, wusste ich
Es besser. Schon seit geraumer Zeit
Hatte ich keine Todesfurcht mehr. Da ja nichts
Mir je fehlen kann, vorausgesetzt
Ich selber fehle. Jetzt
Gelang es mir, mich zu freuen
Alles Amselgesanges nach mir auch.[1] (*GW 9*, p. 1031)

Problems of Interpretation

There are a number of dangers which lie in wait for the critic approaching Brecht's work. Although I shall use the text of the *Gesammelte Werke* for reference purposes, it is necessary to point out that in some respects this text is unsatisfactory and, at times, even confusing. Take, for instance, the case of *Baal*. Thanks to Dieter Schmidt's invaluable work, there are now no fewer than five printed versions of the play available. In many ways, the text of the *Gesammelte Werke* is the least satisfactory, while the 1919 version is the most rewarding for the interpreter. But the problems arise if one seeks to interpret the play in the light of Brecht's own later remarks. In his essay *Bei Durchsicht meiner ersten Stücke* ('On looking through my first plays'), he writes:

> Das Stück *Baal* mag denen, die nicht gelernt haben, dialektisch zu denken, allerhand Schwierigkeiten bereiten. Sie werden darin kaum etwas anderes als die Verherrlichung nackter Ichsucht erblicken.[2] (*GW 17*, p. 947)

Now, even in the *Gesammelte Werke* version, it is difficult to find anything other than a 'Verherrlichung nackter Ichsucht'

---

[1] When in the white sick room at the Charité
I awoke towards morning
And heard the blackbird, I understood
Better. For some time already
I had lost all fear of death. For nothing
Can be wrong with me, provided
I myself am nothing. Now
I managed to enjoy
The song of every blackbird after me as well.

[2] The play *Baal* may present all sorts of difficulties to those who have not learnt to think dialectically. In it they will hardly perceive anything but the glorification of naked egoism.

(glorification of naked egoism), though Brecht made some alterations in an attempt to redress the balance. The alterations are so slight, however, that the moral of the play remains the same: and Brecht himself admits later in the same essay that he lacks the energy necessary to make any drastic changes to the play. Hence, if one were to observe Brecht's admonition to 'think dialectically', one would end up with an interpretation totally at odds with the play itself. Far more helpful, and closer to the truth, is his remark from an earlier draft of the essay, in which he hints at a more positive attitude:

> Die Grundannahme des Stücks ist mir kaum noch zugänglich, jedoch scheint sie mir ein Feld abzugeben, auf dem eine überaus genussvolle Beziehung zur Landschaft, zu menschlichen Verhältnissen erotischer oder halberotischer Art, zur Sprache usw. entstehen kann.[1]

Similar problems occur with *Im Dickicht der Städte* (In the Jungle of Cities) and *Mann ist Mann* (A Man's a Man). In the case of the former, we encounter a situation similar to that outlined above: except that this time a foreword to the play expressly urges the audience and reader towards the attitude Brecht demands:

> Sie betrachten den unerklärlichen Ringkampf zweier Menschen und Sie wohnen dem Untergang einer Familie bei, die aus den Savannen in das Dickicht der grossen Stadt gekommen ist. Zerbrechen Sie sich nicht den Kopf über die Motive dieses Kampfes, sondern beteiligen Sie sich an den menschlichen Einsätzen, beurteilen Sie unparteiisch die Kampfform der Gegener und lenken Sie Ihr Interesse auf das Finish.[2]   (*GW 1*, p. 126)

This would be fine if the plot (as distinct from the play's

---

[1] The play's basic assumption is now scarcely accessible to me, yet it seems to provide a field where a genuinely enjoyable connection with the landscape, with human relationships of an erotic or semi-erotic nature, with language, etc. can be established.

[2] You are observing the inexplicable wrestling match between two human beings and you are present at the downfall of a family which has come from the savannahs into the thicket of the metropolis. Don't rack your brains about the motives for this struggle, but involve yourselves in the human resources employed, judge the fighting style of the combatants impartially and focus your interest on the finish.

structure) could be seen as the stages in a match between two wrestlers. But to see it solely in such terms is to miss the charade-element which is so essential to the plot, and to over-simplify both the character of the protagonists and the nature of the conflict itself. The first version of *Im Dickicht der Städte* was written between 1921 and 1922, whereas the passage from the foreword cited above was written for the version published in 1927. A clear picture of the changes Brecht made to the drama can now be gained from a comparison of the earlier text (now published in an edition by Gisela Bahr) with the later one.

And *Mann ist Mann*? In some ways, this is the most complex of all. Brecht had been drafting out a play concerned with the question of what man can be changed into since 1918. When he took up the play again in the twenties, he introduced a number of other elements, but the basic situation remained. Nevertheless, the printed version, based on the 1938 and 1927 texts, has led some critics into placing undue stress on a socio-economic interpretation rather than one which bases its conclusions on an analysis of the figure of Galy Gay and how he 'bends in the wind'. To see the work merely in anti-capitalistic or anti-militaristic terms, or as a condemnation of the 'false collective' is to disregard the crucial fact that Galy Gay himself is a figure who readily adapts to the demands of the new situation and his new surroundings. An interpretation which looks first at this 'adaptability' and readiness to conform, then at the relationship between him and the other members of the 'group', and finally at the behaviourist elements in the play, will be at once more valid and more helpful for an understanding of Brecht's own development.

The problems outlined above are not so acute in the case of the poetry, in so far as Brecht was not given to such wholesale reworking of his poems. There are, of course, a number which, over the years, were being revised or having stanzas added. But the basic statement is seldom radically altered or distorted by the introduction of extraneous elements which might tempt the critic to see them as the basis for any new interpretation. Clearly, there are exceptions: 'Das Lied von der Eisenbahntruppe von Fort Donald' as printed in the *Hauspostille* (*Manual of Piety*) is, in terms of its language, a different poem from the one that appeared in 1916. This highlights one of the distinctions in Brecht's approach to reworking poems or dramas: in the case of the latter, new thematic elements are frequently introduced, and it is often difficult to separate the earlier from the later stages of work. In the case of the former, it is more often the language and diction to which Brecht devotes his attention, less frequently the structure—though 'Die Moritat von Mackie Messer' ('The Ballad of Mack the Knife') underwent several reworkings over the years, mostly in the form of the alteration, deletion or addition of stanzas. The problem in the case of the poetry is rather more straightforward, though its consequences are crucial: it is the difficulty of dating the poems themselves, and the interpretative pitfalls this represents for the critic.

To take the most obvious instance. It would be wrong to see the *Hauspostille* (published 1927) and the collection *Aus einem Lesebuch für Städtebewohner* (From a Reader for those who Live in Cities) (which Brecht was working on at the same time, i.e. 1926–7), as representing two different directions in the poetry of these years. Almost all the *Hauspostille* poems were written before 1922, and the idea of such a collection had been first mooted then. When the *Hauspostille* finally appeared, Brecht's poetry had already taken a new direction. The themes and forms of the *technisches Zeitalter* (technical age) were demanding his attention and his language had lost much of the extravagant colour and richness which distinguish the *Hauspostille* poems. It is, then, a question of ascertaining the facts before making assumptions about a drama or poem which can easily be shown to be based on false premises. Such a plea for caution should not of course be read as an advocacy for a return to an undifferentiated positivist approach to the interpretation of Brecht's work. But it is as well to bear in mind that the most reliable interpretations—such as the studies of Willett, Grimm, Münsterer and Schmidt—have been so instructive because they have not lost themselves in speculation about Brecht's life, or in applying to his work pre-selected categories which can be shown to be inappropriate and unhelpful. For until the publication of all the material necessary to a complete understanding of his development (such as the diaries and work-books), and the appearance of a full-scale critical biography, it will be possible to give only qualified answers to a number of problems of interpretation. Above all one should resist the temptation to over-simplify the complex development of a writer whose work does not lend itself to the concept of 'linear' or 'organic' development or of the *sudden* discarding of one style in favour of another, with the consequent rejection of all that has gone before. Brecht's own words on this score are worth remembering:

> Es ist keine Frage: die Literatur blüht nicht. Aber man sollte sich hüten, in alten Bildern zu denken. Den Wert, die Bestimmung der Kraft und der Grösse darf man nicht an die idyllische Vorstellung des organischen Blühens fesseln. Das wäre absurd. Abstieg und Aufstieg sind nicht durch Daten im Kalender getrennt. Diese Linien gehen durch Personen und Werke durch.[1] (*ÜL*, p. 75)

[1] There's no question about it: literature does not flower. But one should refrain from thinking in old images. Value, and the establishing of force and greatness should not be chained to the idyllic notion of organic flowering. That would be absurd. Decline and ascent are not separated by dates in the calendar. These lines run right through people and works.

2

Early Plays

Baal

Brecht's early dramas have a number of thematic elements in common: man versus nature and/or society; the problem of isolation either as a state chosen by the individual or thrust upon him by others; the outsider who makes his own rules; the vitality and tenacity which allow him to come out on top. Admittedly, such a view entails seeing victory even in Baal's death—but this is completely in keeping with the tenor of the play. There is even a hint of something not far removed from a Christian acceptance of the necessity and inevitability of death —but Baal's (and his author's) attitude is deliberately perverted and radically different from the quasi-mystical philosophy of other Expressionist works. Where Georg Kaiser's heroes might well have cried, with arms outstretched and head flung back: 'Death where is thy sting, or grave thy victory?' Baal knows from the outset that any sting death may have had is long since blunted. It is a fact of existence which he accepts with a shrug of the shoulders. He does not need to defy death in flights of language: his very mode of existence is the clearest expression of his defiance. The same defiance is reflected in his own poetry and in his view of its (and his) role; for he is hardly a lyric poet of the kind best fitted to lend distinction to literary salons. He is a coarse, brutal sensualist, fond of drink and women. In a series of open-ended scenes Brecht presents Baal in a variety of situations: at a society party, in a café performing his own songs, in bed in his attic with various women. His only close friend is Ekart, with whom he has a love–hate relationship, full of homosexual undertones. In the later sections of the play the two roam the countryside together until, after eight years, Baal stabs him in a brawl. At the end we find Baal alone in a woodcutter's hut in the forest, crawling out into the night for a last look at the stars before he dies.

In death, Baal loses nothing; he is not defeated or destroyed, merely restored to the nature whence he came. He embodies all those qualities which distinguish the heroes of the early poetry —their lust for life, their refusal to surrender in their struggle against nature, their position as outcasts. The play itself owes much of its force to the dynamic vitality of its central figure, and to the conviction which the young Brecht brings to his characterization of Baal. Author and character set out to assert the truth of Wedekind's philosophy, expressed in *Schloss Wetterstein* (Castle Wetterstein), that 'das Fleisch hat seinen eigenen Geist' (The flesh has its own mind). There are, of course, weaknesses: the loose construction is unwieldy and is not handled with the skill of the mature dramas, and the whole work suffers somewhat from the lack of a clearly thought-out plot. But it is rather unfair to criticize the lack of plot in a drama which is primarily concerned with viewing the world and the experiences it has to offer from the standpoint of the principal character. It is a drama which depends on establishing a specific emotional atmosphere which corresponds to the various moods of Baal himself; and the mock-rhapsodic title 'Baal frisst! Baal tanzt!! Baal verklärt sich!!!' ('Baal makes a pig of himself! Baal dances!! Baal is transfigured!!!')—which Brecht gave the play at an earlier stage of composition—provides a clear pointer to the combination of action and character which govern the play's course.

It is missing the point to look for development or change in Baal himself: his character is established from the very beginning, and the course of his life clearly charted in the 'Choral vom grossen Baal':

Als im weissen Mutterschosse aufwuchs Baal
War der Himmel schon so gross and still und fahl
Jung und nackt und ungeheuer wundersam
Wie ihn Baal dann liebte, als Baal kam.
* * *

Als im dunklen Erdenschosse faulte Baal
War der Himmel noch so gross und still und fahl
Jung und nackt und ungeheuer wunderbar
Wie ihn Baal einst liebte, als Baal war.[1]

(GW 1, pp. 3–4)

The circular motion of the play is accentuated by the repetition of the image of the heavens: the passage from life to death and the connection of the two is encompassed by the notions of growth (*aufwuchs*) and decay (*faulte*): the indifference of nature to man's presence and its unchanging aspect are both caught in two simple words (*schon* and *noch*): and the feeling of regularity and inevitability is heightened by the uniformity of the syntax and rhythm. The drama presents a pattern of behaviour, a series of experiences, and Baal reacts to each situation in a way which is completely in keeping with what we learn of his character in the opening scene of the play. Judged by any normal standards, he is amoral, asocial and destructive. He has opted out of society and seeks to experience life at all levels and under all circumstances. Unlike the hero of the conventional Expressionist *Stationendrama* (Station drama), which charted its hero's progress along the path to eventual self-awareness and a type of spiritual transcendence, Brecht's anti-hero is well aware of his instincts from the beginning. Yet in terms of its structure, Brecht's play follows Baal's progress in much the same way that Kaiser's *Von Morgens bis Mitternachts* (From Morning to Midnight) follows the movements of the little bank clerk. The mood of the play, however, intended as it was as a rejoinder to Hanns Johst's *Der Einsame* (The Lonely One), is deliberately at odds with the outwardly traditional Expressionist structure. It is more grotesque, at times savagely ironic, and the language,

---

[1] When Baal grew within the maternal womb so white
Up above the sky was vast and calm and light
Naked and young and oh so marvellous
As Baal loved it when Baal came to us.

* * *

When Baal rotted in the dark terrestrial womb
Up above the sky was vast and calm and light
Naked and young and oh so wonderful
As Baal loved it when Baal was with us.

with its alternating passages of violent sensuality and muted lyricism is unlike the unrelievedly rhetorical style normally associated with Expressionist drama.

Moreover, at the same time as Baal is being shown at various stages of his existence, we are always intended to be aware that the *Stationen* (stations)—essentially a linear movement—are a part of the larger *ewiger Kreislauf* (eternal cycle) of life and nature. It is from his own awareness of himself as part of this birth–experience–death cycle that Baal derives his *Lebensziel* (aim in life). Once he has accepted the view that 'in my end is my beginning' (or vice versa)—the biblical phraseology is not accidental—then his life has a purpose. Its purpose lies in a paradoxical affirmation of the value of life, which is far removed from the nihilistic view of existence propagated by some Expressionists. Perhaps the clearest statement of this philosophy of life (which Brecht shares with his characters) is contained in two poems from the same period—the 'Grosser Dankchoral' ('The Great Hymn of Thanksgiving') and 'Gegen Verführung' ('Against Temptation'). In the latter, originally entitled 'Luzifers Abendlied' ('Lucifer's Evening Song'), the poet, in the role of a sardonic devil's advocate, offers advice and exhortation to man which use Christian and religious phraseology but turn the traditional beliefs upside down. The former is an ironic hymn of thanksgiving for all the natural and even 'negative' aspects of life on earth—grass, the animals, carrion, darkness. And the final stanzas of both poems present the logical corollary to this belief in the here and now in preference to the hereafter:

> Lobet die Kälte, die Finsternis und das Verderben!
> Schauet hinan:
> Es kommet nicht auf euch an
> Und ihr könnt unbesorgt sterben.[1]   (*GW 8*, p. 216)

* * *

[1] Praise ye the cold, the dark and the decomposition!
Look all around:
You're a thing of no worth
And you can die without qualms.

Lasst euch nicht verführen!
Zu Fron und Ausgezehr!
Was kann euch Angst noch rühren?
Ihr sterbt mit allen Tieren
Und es kommt nichts nachher.[1]   (ibid., p. 260)

As for the play's structure: already we see Brecht choosing
the arrangement according to scenes (rather than the traditional structure in acts) which is to become typical of the later
works. *Baal* consists of twenty-two scenes of varying length,
written for the most part in heightened prose, four songs and
scattered fragments of songs, and the introductory chorale.
The scenes are loosely strung together, though they do not
display the non-developmental pattern which is evolved in the
mature dramas. Similarly, the role of the songs is somewhat
different from their function in the later dramas, in that they
are more integrated into the action of each particular scene,
and make no attempt to break or relativize the mood of the
scene in which they occur.

Trommeln in der Nacht (Drums in the Night)

Brecht returns to the traditional five-act structure with his next
play, the 'comedy' *Trommeln in der Nacht*. But even here, he
modifies the structure of the traditional comedy. It is more
common to use the three-act construction for comedy (though
there are obviously exceptions to this): Brecht makes use of a
five-act layout which is traditionally associated with tragedy.
Furthermore, the specific and terse scene-captions which pre-
cede each act (*Afrika*; *Pfeffer* (Pepper); *Walkürenritt* (Ride
of the Valkyrie); *Es kommt ein Morgenrot* (A new dawn is
coming); *Das Bett* (The Bed)) are not what one might expect:
an obvious irony is added to their atmospheric, symbolic and
localizing functions. The hero, Kragler, is again an anti-hero

---

[1] Do not let them tempt you!
  Into travail and drudgery!
  Why be affected by fear?
  You die with the beasts of the earth
  And there is nothing hereafter.

just as Baal was, though without the latter's energy and dominating personality.

The setting for the play is Berlin at the time of the 'Spartakus' uprising in January 1919, following on from the November revolution of the previous year—the time of the first version of the work. Anna Balicke is engaged to Andreas Kragler who has been away at the war—fighting in Africa (!)—for four years. Against her wishes, her family finally forces her to accede to the advances of the capitalist Murk, and she becomes pregnant by him. But Andreas's sudden return throws the plans for the alliance with Murk into disarray: both Murk and the Balickes are suspicious of Andreas because of his past, his volatility and their conviction that he is linked with the forces of the revolution. This conviction turns out to be false; for, given the choice between the false bourgeois idyll of existence with the Balickes of this world, and involvement with the revolution, Andreas turns his back on the proletariat and goes off with his 'sullied bride' into the world of hypocrisy and double standards. Yet he remains his own man, impervious to the reactions of those around him, especially to the enthusiasm of others like himself who are ready to die for an idea. The later Brecht may well condemn Kragler as a 'kleiner Realist' (little realist) and 'meuternder Kleinbürgersoldat' (mutinous petit bourgeois soldier) but it is obvious from the play that Kragler's cynicism and small-minded sense of priorities are not qualities easily brushed aside. Part of the explanation for the play's positive presentation of the character of Kragler can be found in *his* awareness of his own shortcomings. Were he to see his actions as morally defensible and indicative of his own superior insight into the situation, and were he to defend these in such terms, one would easily adopt a more negative attitude towards him. But that mocking cynicism which refuses to spare others does not hesitate to direct its gaze at himself. When at the end of the play Kragler declares: 'Ich bin ein Schwein, und das Schwein geht heim' (I'm a pig, and the pig goes home), it is the logical conclusion to that view of himself, expressed in images of animals and physical and spiritual disfigurement which he has put forward throughout the play.

Im Dickicht der Städte (In the Jungle of Cities)

By far the most complex and enigmatic of the early dramas is *Im Dickicht der Städte*. Where Baal puts himself outside society and chooses the fields, the woods and a debased 'back-to-nature' philosophy, this pattern is reversed in the case of George Garga. He has left nature's jungle for the human zoo of Chicago: and at the end of the play he is about to set out on an expedition for the even more impenetrable and enveloping thicket of the metropolis of New York. In the closing lines of the play he pronounces in three lapidary sentences the last rites over an attitude to existence which he shares with all the central figures of Brecht's early work:

> Allein sein ist eine gute Sache. Das Chaos ist aufgebraucht.
> Es war die beste Zeit.[1]   (*GW 1*, p. 193)

It is a strangely tranquil and even nostalgic ending to a play in which violence and destruction lurk in the shadows, and in which the menacing riddles of language, reflecting the puzzle of life, so clearly anticipate the Theatre of the Absurd.

The reasons for the struggle between Shlink and Garga are difficult to pin down. The initial sparring for an opening comes at the very beginning of Scene 1, with Shlink, the Malayan timber merchant, involving Garga in an argument for no apparent reason. When the confrontation results in the demolition of the bookshop where Garga works and his subsequent dismissal, he accepts the struggle. Yet within a short time we find him contemplating an escape to Tahiti in order to be free of the entanglement with Shlink. At this point Shlink forces Garga to reject this plan by involving his family in the affair—he succeeds in making prostitutes of Garga's sister Marie and his girlfriend Jane. Driving home the advantage he now has, he sees to it that Garga is sent to jail and the family itself broken up. The motivation for these events remains obscure and the picture becomes even more clouded when Garga, on his release from jail, revenges himself on Shlink by bringing against him a charge of raping his sister. When a lynching

---

[1] Being alone is a good thing. The chaos is used up. It was the best time.

mob threatens to seize Shlink, Garga and he flee together into the countryside round Lake Michigan, where in the auspicious surroundings of a quarry, Shlink hands over to Garga his re-built timber business and confesses his love for him. Garga rejects Shlink; the latter takes poison before the mob reaches him, Garga burns the timber yard to the ground and sets off for New York.

Behind Shlink's attack and his wish to do battle with Garga lies a force akin to Iago's 'motiveless malignity'—though Shlink feels no hatred for Garga. This 'motivelessness' is a quality of which Brecht was well aware: in the 1928 intro-duction to the play we find him emphasizing to his audience that human patterns of behaviour are no longer explicable in terms of 'motives' which owe more to literature than to real life. Suppositions can now be shown to be false, certain types of character act contrary to accepted norms; it is the behaviour itself rather than the reasons for this behaviour which must occupy the dramatist's and audience's attention. These ob-servations clearly owe much to Brecht's own preoccupation at the time with behaviourist ideas, and hence cannot be taken as the final word on a play whose genesis antedates its author's interest in behaviourism. At the same time they help to clarify those elements in the play in which Brecht has anticipated his later sociological studies. His own attitude to the work is un-equivocal:

> In dieser Welt und in dieser Dramatik findet sich der Philosoph besser zurecht als der Psychologe.[1]
>
> (*GW 17*, p. 970)

But this instruction is more effective as an epigram than as an interpretative diagram.

The subject of the play is the violent struggle between two individuals, a 'Kampf an sich' (the struggle per se): but it is impossible to overlook the various conflicting reasons for entering into the struggle which the *text* advances, and which motivate Shlink in particular. Even Marie Garga sees that

---

[1] In this world and in this dramatic art the philosopher will be more at home than the psychologist.

Shlink is a complex and inscrutable figure (he is not an Oriental for nothing!):

> Ich verstehe Sie schlecht, Mr Shlink. Aber Sie können nach vier Richtungen gehen, wo andere nur eine haben, nicht? Ein Mensch hat viele Möglichkeiten, nicht? Ich sehe, ein Mensch hat viele Möglichkeiten.[1]
>
> (*GW 1*, p. 144)

Another of Shlink's reasons for seeking the test of strength with Garga is his sense of isolation in the city, what he himself calls 'die unendliche Vereinzelung des Menschen' (the infinite isolation of the human being). Not even language or the normal patterns of communication can counter this isolation which is basically an existential rather than a social predicament. Shlink decides that the only way of establishing contact is by throwing out a challenge which cannot be disregarded as easily as an offer of friendship. In Shlink's challenge and the relationship he hopes for with Garga, love is mixed not with hatred but with curiosity as to how the adversary will react to the 'no-holds-barred' contest. He has no real quarrel with Garga, only a wish to bind him to himself in a relationship which is by no means free of its homosexual aspects. The play deals in a more ambivalent fashion with the problem of the homosexual relationship between two men which occurs also in *Baal*, *Bargan lässt es sein*, 'Ballade von der Freundschaft' (Ballad of Friendship) and *Leben Eduards des Zweiten* (The Life of Edward II). Brecht's first treatment of the theme was prompted by his interest in the Verlaine–Rimbaud relationship, but each of the above-mentioned instances considers the theme from a slightly altered viewpoint.

Throughout the play Brecht links the language and images of love and friendship with images of violence and cruelty: the combination mirrors the nature of the conflict itself. For Shlink the fight is all-important. And there are moments in the play when—dare one suggest?—it would come as no surprise to hear him cry 'This thing is bigger than both of us!' (He would,

---

[1] I have difficulty in understanding you, Mr Shlink. But you can go in four directions, where others only have one, right? A human being has many possibilities, right? I can see, a human being has many possibilities.

of course, be speaking—at least in the first instance—of the fight.) Such an analogy between a love-relationship and the fight which ties Garga to Shlink is not inappropriate. In the same way that the two partners in a love-relationship will have different demands and expectations, so too the wishes of Garga and Shlink do not coincide. No measure of agreement can be reached on what each seeks from the fight. Shlink sees it as a way of establishing contact, and hints that he would welcome an expression of interest on Garga's part in his reasons for choosing this course. But Garga is not in the least interested in *why* Shlink has come to him:

> *Garga:* . . . Ich werde mit Ihnen reinen Tisch machen. (*Den Revolver in der Hand*): Auge um Auge, Zahn um Zahn.
> *Shlink:* Sie nehmen den Kampf auf?
> *Garga:* Ja! Natürlich unverbindlich.
> *Shlink:* Und ohne nach dem Grund zu fragen?
> *Garga:* Ohne nach dem Grund zu fragen. Ich mag nicht wissen, wozu Sie einen Kampf nötig haben. Sicher ist der Grund faul. Für mich genügt es, dass Sie sich für den besseren Mann halten.[1] (GW *1*, p. 138)

In the final exchanges between the two, each for the first time reveals his own reasons for accepting the struggle; and it is clear that it was doomed to failure from the beginning:

> *Shlink:* . . . Sie haben nicht begriffen, was es war. Sie wollten mein Ende, aber ich wollte den Kampf. Nicht das Körperliche, sondern das Geistige war es.
> *Garga:* Und das Geistige, das sehen Sie, das ist nichts. Es ist nicht wichtig, der Stärkere zu sein, sondern der Lebendige. Ich kann Sie nicht besiegen, ich kann Sie nur in den Boden stampfen.[2] (*GW 1*, p. 190)

[1] *Garga:* I'll finish you off properly. (*With gun in hand*): An eye for an eye, a tooth for a tooth.
Shlink: You accept the struggle?
Garga: Yes! And of course, under no duress.
Shlink: And without asking for the reason?
Garga: Without asking for the reason. I do not wish to know why you need a struggle. The reason is bound to be rotten. It's enough for me that you think yourself the better man.
[2] *Shlink:* You didn't understand what it was. You wanted to finish me, but I wanted the struggle. Nothing physical; it was spiritual.

Even in the initial sparring, Shlink had already assumed a position of inferiority: victory was not his aim, and his deliberate self-abasement is expressed in words whose masochistic and sexual overtones can be clearly heard:

> *Shlink:* . . . Mein Haus und mein Holzhandel zum Beispiel setzen mich instand, Ihnen die Hunde auf den Hals zu jagen. Geld ist alles. Gut. Aber mein Haus ist das Ihrige, dieser Holzhandel gehört Ihnen. Von heute ab, Mr Garga, lege ich mein Geschick in Ihre Hände. Sie sind mir unbekannt. Von heute ab bin ich Ihre Kreatur. Jeder Blick Ihrer Augen wird mich beunruhigen. Jeder Ihrer Wünsche, auch der unbekannte, wird mich willfährig finden. Ihre Sorge ist meine Sorge, meine Kraft wird die Ihre sein.[1]   (*GW 1*, p. 138)

It is no accident that the last sentence sounds like a parody of the marriage vows—implied also is the understanding that this union will be life-long. In the end, though death finally severs the bond between the two, Garga has already turned his back on the contest before Shlink commits suicide. Both, in effect, throw in the towel, and the distance between them remains as great at the end as it was at the beginning. Not only have they never really come to blows, they were never even fighting each other—merely engaging in shadow-boxing.

The play abounds with references ranging from the obvious to the recherché and the positively arcane. There are direct quotations from Rimbaud's *Une Saison en Enfer*; echoes of Whitman and Schiller's *Die Räuber* (The Brigands); borrowings from and references to: J. V. Jensen's novel *Das Rad* (The Wheel) (whose Chicago setting and theme of a struggle

---

Garga: And the spiritual, you can now see, is nothing. It's not important to be the stronger, but to be the one who's alive. I can't conquer you, I can only grind you into the dust.

[1] *Shlink:* . . . My house and my timber trade for example, put me in the position of being able to set the dogs on you. Money is everything. Good. But my house is your house, this timber yard belongs to you. From today, Mr Garga, I place my fate in your hands. You are not known to me. From today I am your creature. Each glance from your eyes will disturb me. Each of your wishes, even the unknown one, will find me compliant. Your cares are my cares, my strength will be yours.

to the death are reflected in the play): the Old Testament (most obvious of which is the repeated image of 'an eye for an eye and a tooth for a tooth'); the New Testament (Shlink deals in wood, Christ was a carpenter—an ironic analogy); and Plato (the death of Shlink is described in words which recall the death of Socrates). Some of these references and analogies are more obvious in the earlier version in which Brecht systematically develops an amalgam of styles. He sets extremes side by side, mixes disparate stylistic (and thematic) elements together in a remarkable demonstration of language (and characters) at cross-purposes. His own description of this procedure is revealing:

> Ich stellte Wortmischungen zusammen wie scharfe Getränke, ganze Szenen in sinnlich empfindbaren Wörtern bestimmter Stofflichkeit und Farbe. Kirschkern, Revolver, Hosentasche, Papiergott: Mischungen von der Art.[1] (*GW 17*, p. 950)

This 'imagistic' approach to language is still clear even in the 1928 version and the procedure outlined above is exemplified by the following passage:

> *Garga:* . . . Ich komme, um dem Burschen ins Gesicht zu blicken, der mir vor zwei Wochen einen kleinen Kirschkern ins Auge spuckte. Ich habe einen Revolver in der Hosentasche. Ich begegne einer zurückweichenden Verbeugung. Er bietet mir seinen Holzhandel an. Ich verstehe nichts, aber ich nehme an. Ich bin allein in der Prärie und kann nichts für dich tun, Ma.
>
> *Der Wurm (von hinten zu ihnen):* Er spielt wie der Papiergott. Ich schwöre, er spielt falsch.[2]
>
> (*GW 1*, pp. 140–1)

---

[1] I mixed words up together like pungent cocktails, whole scenes of words of a definite substance and colour that could be experienced sensuously. Cherry pip, revolver, trouser pocket, paper God: mixtures like that.

[2] *Garga:* I come to look the fellow straight in the face who two weeks back spat a tiny cherry pip in my eye. I have a revolver in my trouser pocket. I meet with a bow and a withdrawal. He offers me his timber yard. I understand nothing, but I accept. I'm alone on the prairie and can do nothing for you, Ma.

Worm (from the back, to them): He plays like the paper God. I'll swear, he's cheating.

It is this sort of impressionistic treatment of dialogue which accounts for some of the play's most obscure and apparently inconsequential passages. The range of styles and variety of imagery are bundled together to produce not an ordered mosaic but a vast, incomplete jigsaw puzzle.

One of the most ingenious instances of Brecht's technique of superimposing various levels of meaning is the opening scene of the play. The exchange between shop-assistant and customer (usually known as 'the dissatisfied customer gag') is one of the stock devices of the silent comedy, a ploy used to brilliant and destructive effect by Chaplin, and, to a lesser degree, by Keaton. It was also a situation particularly favoured by Karl Valentin in his extravagant and zany sketches: the misunderstanding between assistant and customer leads to a conclusion in which confusion and absurdity run riot. But it is a conclusion which is the natural and inevitable outcome of the inverted logic and out-of-focus reasoning which Valentin employed. In a typical silent comedy, Shlink might have gone to a tailor's to buy a suit, and after a series of mishaps, decided that the one he really wanted was the one Garga was wearing. Brecht's Shlink enters a lending library and seeks to buy Garga's opinions—a situation essentially just as farcical and illogical, but imbued here with a sense of menace and uneasiness which is occasionally hinted at in Chaplin's films, but which is not so integral a part of the work itself. The slapstick and knockabout elements in *Im Dickicht der Städte* are an essential part of the play's atmosphere, just as essential as the more serious problems the play treats. Even the figure of Shlink himself owes something to the twenties vogue for the thriller centred round the figure of a mysterious and menacing Chinese. (Significantly enough Brecht tries to hide Shlink's origins by making him a Malay, but the constant references in the text to his 'yellow skin' make the connection with Fu Manchu, Charlie Chan and the Tongs quite clear.) Far from being merely trivial, such elements are an essential part of the play's world of paradoxes.

3

Survival and Social Involvement

Mann ist Mann (A Man's a Man)

In the first scene of *Im Dickicht der Städte*, Shlink invites Garga to venture an opinion: he refuses, saying that he is prepared to sell the views and attitudes of an author, but that his opinions are his own. Throughout the play he strives to retain an individuality and sense of independence which will allow him to continue with this luxury. But in *Mann ist Mann*, Galy Gay (who bears more than a superficial resemblance to George Garga) loses all individuality; it is even arguable that from the beginning he has no individual personality. The process begun in *Im Dickicht der Städte* is completed with the transformation of the packer Galy Gay into a fighting machine. Where Garga refuses to sell his own opinion, Galy Gay, in Brecht's own words, 'Kann sich sogar nur selten eine eigene Meinung gestatten' (can only seldom allow himself even the luxury of a personal opinion) (*GW 17*, p. 978). But just as Garga—for different reasons—finds himself unable to reject Shlink's offer of the fight, so too, Galy Gay is all too ready to accede to the persuasion of others. A man who cannot say no, he sets out one morning to buy a fish for his wife; but this apparently simple task brings with it a chain of complications. On the way he falls among thieves—in this case, three soldiers of the British Colonial Army who have just looted a pagoda. Afraid that the absence of the fourth member of the gang, who had been left behind during the raid, might throw suspicion on them, they persuade Galy Gay to stand in for him at roll-call. The deception succeeds, but when they attempt to convince him to continue with the pretence, he declines. (By now the fourth soldier has become a miracle-working deity in the

pagoda, and the priest refuses to release him.) Gradually,
however, the three break down Galy Gay's resistance by involving him in an elaborate charade in which he auctions a fake
elephant. They finally turn on him, accuse him of fraud and
lead him before a fake firing squad. Terrified, Galy Gay collapses in a faint, and on recovering, declares himself to be the
missing soldier Jeraiah Jip, and delivers a funeral oration over
his own body. The final scenes show the complete transformation: the fighting machine Gay/Jip becomes the embodiment
of the military spirit as he leads the army off to war and single-
handed captures a fortress.

It is again a question of 'the survival of the fittest', a theme
which appears in one form or other in almost every one of
Brecht's dramas. Whether it be the adaptability of Galy Gay,
the acceptance of the ritual of the 'Talwurf' (casting down
into the valley) in *Der Jasager* (He who says yes), the fondness
for the good things in life which leads Galileo to recant, or
Shen Te's assumption of the role of Shui Ta to allow her to
exist in the face of the exploitation by others, the problem of
survival and/or the sacrifices it entails is a theme which occupied
Brecht from the very beginning. It is significant that one of the
earliest explicit statements of this theme (which derives initially
from Darwin and materialism) is to be found in a song from
the first version of *Im Dickicht der Städte*:

> Drei Freunde, die legten den vierten ins Grab,
> Den Moder im Mund, die Erd' im Gesicht;
> Zogen hinauf nach dem Norden, nach dem Süden
>   hinab—
> Der kranke Mann stirbt, und der starke Mann ficht.[1]

But it is not Brecht's reading of Darwin which leads him to
incorporate these lines in the play—nor indeed any new-found
interest in the principles of materialism. It is his reading of
Kipling: for the lines above, together with a second stanza,
occur at the beginning of Chapter 12 of *The Light That Failed*,

---

[1] Three friends they laid the fourth in a grave
Decay in his mouth, earth in his face;
Set out for the North, and off down to the South
The sick man dies and the strong man fights.

and the last line was to re-appear in the merchant's song from
Die Ausnahme und die Regel (The Exception and the Rule).
It could equally well serve as motto for the death and subsequent transformation of Galy Gay. And the situation the song
describes is reflected in the plot of *Mann ist Mann*, where the
three comrades 'bury' a fourth, resurrect him and all march off
to the North. It is no coincidence that this work, which of all
Brecht's dramas owes most to his reading of Kipling, should
provide one of the most bizarre illustrations of Kipling's maxim
that 'the strong man fights and the sick man dies'.

One must, however, qualify the above observations. Galy
Gay is hardly the supreme embodiment of the will to survive:
he is closer to the idea of the *Gummimensch* (india-rubber man),
who will bounce back. He is a comic, sometimes pathetically
bewildered figure, who is unable to understand either the fact
of, or the reasons for his manipulation by others. Yet although
Galy Gay is usually being acted upon, rather than behaving in
accordance with his own initial impulses, Brecht does not intend
us to view this as an essentially negative situation. Nor indeed
is his inability to say no such a critical failing—at least within
the play itself. In 1927, when Brecht was more concerned with
giving the comic elements in the play their due, he could proffer
the following advice to the audience of a radio production:

> Ich denke auch, Sie sind gewohnt, einen Menschen, der
> nicht nein sagen kann, als einen Schwächling zu be-
> trachten, aber dieser Galy Gay ist gar kein Schwächling,
> im Gegenteil, er ist der Stärkste. Er ist allerdings erst
> der Stärkste, nachdem er aufgehört hat, eine Privat-
> person zu sein, er wird erst in der Masse stark.[1]
>
> (*GW 17*, p. 978)

The temptation even now is to view the play as a bleak illustration of the 'Untergang des Menschen in der Masse' (extinc-
tion of the human being in the masses) and to see Galy Gay

[1] I would also think that you are accustomed to consider a person who
cannot say no to be a weakling, but this Galy Gay is far from being a weakling; on the contrary, he's the strongest. Granted, he is the strongest only
after he has ceased to be a private individual; only in the mass does he become strong.

throughout as a genuinely pathetic figure who is overcome by
forces he cannot understand or control. This is not to say that
such elements are absent from the play, but they are set side
by side with incidents that illustrate nothing so much as
Brecht's fondness for a type of slapstick lunacy that may very
well anticipate the more bizarre world of the Absurd, but
which is closer to the knockabout comedy of the circus and
the beer-hall.

Die Dreigroschenoper (The Threepenny Opera) and the Attack on the Middle Class

The later stages of the work on *Mann ist Mann* coincided with
Brecht's increasing awareness of social questions and the beginnings of his interest in Marxism. Though this new direction
in his work is more apparent in the poetry from this time, the
language and theme of *Mann ist Mann* also point forward rather
than back. The play stands at the crossroads; the plot incorpor-
ates thematic features already familiar from the early dramas,
but Brecht's style and his treatment of these features reflect his
own interest in a more socially orientated view of the world.
But within the context of his work the next full-length play
Die Dreigroschenoper represents a step back rather than a
move forward towards the incorporation of Marxist ideas
and principles. This is not the same as saying that such
ideas would have materially improved the work—quite the
contrary. If the *Dreigroschenroman* (Threepenny Novel) is
anything to go by, they would have ensured its immediate
failure. But at the time Brecht needed a success, and although
some subsequent studies have sought to play down the com-
mercialism and audience-appeal element of *Die Dreigroschenoper*, it becomes increasingly apparent that the work was
little more than a pot-boiler—though indeed one of the most
successful pot-boilers in the history of the German theatre.

Many of the songs, which are the work's most appealing
feature, were rescued from the bottom of Brecht's drawer and
the play was built around them. Even though John Gay's
Beggar's Opera was used as a framework, the resulting non-

sequiturs and shapelessness cannot be explained by saying that the construction is typical of Brecht's 'scenic' rather than 'organic' approach. The plot comes a poor fourth behind the music, the songs and the characters—though these too tend to become mere vehicles for the songs.

This is borne out by a revealing anecdote concerning one of the best-known of the work's showpieces, 'Die Seeräuber-Jenny' ('Pirate Jenny') which, in most performances, and in the *GW* edition, is sung by Polly Peachum. Kurt Weill's wife, Lotte Lenya, had been cast in the minor role of Spelunken-Jenny, and had been given no big number in the first part. Weill demanded she be given the 'Seeräuber-Jenny' number, to which Brecht agreed—whereupon Carola Neher (who was playing Polly), furious that the number had been taken from her, threw the role in Brecht's face and walked out—some ten days before the opening performance. This would be merely another anecdote, were it not for the fact that Brecht clearly felt few qualms in lifting a song out of context and giving it to another character. And this is hardly surprising, since the song was never written with the character of Polly (or indeed anyone) in mind! The evidence for this can be found in the Brecht-Archiv, where the text of the song, in an arrangement by F. S. Bruinier, is dated 8 March 1927. Even more interesting is the music itself, which bears a striking resemblance to Weill's later setting; indeed, the refrain is identical. Here is the first direct confirmation of what some critics have always felt—that Weill's musical style, in those works written with Brecht, owes more to the latter than was initially apparent. This is not to belittle Weill's achievement in *Dreigroschenoper* or *Happy End*. The music displays a consistently high level of wit and imagination, together with a quite unique feeling for melody and rhythmic vitality. And Weill's gift for musical parody still sounds sharp and refreshing, while nowadays the satire in the play itself falls rather flat. Such satire as there was, was never particularly stinging—the bourgeois audiences (with Brecht's partial connivance) lapped it up and came back for more. But the songs retain their bite, and remain as vigorous as ever. This is due to two factors: the text is both more apt and more forceful than most of the play's piecemeal dialogue, and the music itself is ideally suited to the task of putting the text across with the necessary wit and drive.

Judged either by the standards of the plays that preceded it or of those that were to follow, *Dreigroschenoper* seems a second-rate work. Even Brecht's own efforts to secure a more significant status for it seem rather unconvincing. To claim as he did in 1931 that:

> Die *Dreigroschenoper* befasst sich mit den bürgerlichen Vorstellungen nicht nur als Inhalt, indem sie diese darstellt, sondern auch durch die Art, wie sie sie dar-stellt.[1] (*GW 17*, p. 991)

is merely an exercise in *ex post facto* Marxist reasoning. The play does attack the middle-class ethic, and it seeks to expose bourgeois society by viewing the world of Peachum and Brown in the same light as it does the underworld of Macheath and his men. But it is an equation too easily drawn up, and drawn up, one suspects, more for reasons of theatrical effectiveness than for any Marxist interpretation of the social implications. Closer to the truth is Brecht's comment in 1929:

> Was die *Dreigroschenoper* betrifft, so ist sie—wenn nichts anderes—eher ein Versuch, der völligen Verblödung der Oper entgegenzuwirken.[2] (*GW 17*, p. 990)

It is tempting to view the work merely as a piece of operetta-like entertainment but, unlike the traditional German operetta, it does have a point to make, and Brecht, with judicious selection from Villon and Kipling, does his best to make it.

Mahagonny

Aufstieg und Fall der Stadt Mahagonny (Rise and Fall of the City of Mahagonny) is a more important work, and Brecht's

---

[1] *The Threepenny Opera* is concerned with bourgeois notions not only as content, in that it presents these, but also through the way in which it presents them.

[2] As far as *The Threepenny Opera* is concerned, it is—if nothing else—rather an attempt to counteract the trend towards making the opera totally idiotic.

only really successful attempt at 'grand opera'. But the plot is hardly typical of the genre. The widow Begbick and two fellow crooks are fleeing from the police somewhere near the Gulf of Mexico and find themselves in the middle of nowhere when their car breaks down. Begbick suggests they found a city to be called Mahagonny, where all those on the search for gold shall be caught as in a net. Paul Ackermann and his friends arrive from Alaska to buy themselves the Mahagonny brand of happiness, and it is round his decline and fall that the plot revolves. After a time life becomes dull, customers start leaving, prices are falling because of a surfeit of *Zufriedenheit* (satisfaction) and prohibitions are being made. However, providence in the unlikely shape of a hurricane intervenes: it veers away from the city at the last moment and the inhabitants come to the conclusion that from now on anything at all is permissible—provided money is available. A year passes and brings further chaos: Paul has run out of money and when Jenny (the whore he loves), turns him down, he is tried, condemned and executed. The work ends with the city burning and torn apart by disorder: and the message is that the lack of money is the root of all 'evil'.

This muddled, if uncompromising, attack on the ethos of capitalism accounts in part for the work's comparative lack of popularity even among devotees of twentieth-century opera; and its music, more complex and 'operatic' than that of *Dreigroschenoper* or *Happy End*, finds few supporters among those used to the more accessible style of those works. Judged by the standards of, for instance, *Wozzeck*, Weill's music lacks the horrifying intensity and profoundly moving sombreness of Berg's score. But the orchestration is stylish, the quality of Weill's invention never flags, and the parodies of grand opera, the references to jazz, the blues, Bach, Strauss and Stravinsky are never introduced as mere gimmickry. Furthermore, to dismiss it as displaying a lack of knowledge of operatic style is not only inaccurate but positively perverse. The writing displays a sure command of vocal line, the set pieces are well integrated, and the characterization is at least as credible as is Strauss's in *Die Frau ohne Schatten* (The Woman without a Shadow) or

Stravinsky's in *Oedipus Rex*. When *Mahagonny* is being criticized for being static, or dull or unconvincing, the real reason is to be sought elsewhere—usually in the critic's rejection of the opera's theme and its eclectic style. It is no more static and unconvincing than a number of modern operas —in fact, as both Brecht and Weill were concerned with following the basic requirements of the operatic genre, they inserted recitatives and arias with the intention of emphasizing the static moments. Furthermore, a work could hardly be considered dull in which a city is devastated by a hurricane, in which one of the most memorable scenes takes place in a queue outside a brothel, in which consecutive scenes show a boxing match, a drunken imaginary voyage to Alaska on a billiard-table, a frenetic court scene and an apocalyptic execution.

If *Mahagonny* is not quite the success it might have been, then the reason is to be found elsewhere: firstly, in its avowedly experimental nature and secondly in its (even now) unpalatable theme. As Brecht declared, the work is '. . . ein Versuch in der epischen Oper: ein Sittenschilderung' (an essay in the form of the epic opera: a presentation of morals and manners) (*GW* 2, p. 1*). The revolutionary reappraisal of the *function* of the opera which Brecht was concerned with at the time was not matched by an awareness on his part of the limitations of the genre, nor, perhaps, by a more intensive study of the experiments of Honegger, Hindemith, Stravinsky and Berg. Indeed, although he had a wide-ranging knowledge of both contemporary and traditional European drama, it appears that—apart from some of Wagner's operas—he was familiar with very few works of the operatic repertoire. Probably he was repelled by the bourgeois values associated with and reflected in the traditional Wagnerian opera: but, far more than the dramatist, the operatic librettist and composer are subject to limitations when it comes to seeking out a totally new theme or subject. If, as Brecht himself declared, 'Der Grad des Genusses hängt direkt vom Grad der Irrealität ab' (The degree of enjoyment is directly dependent on the degree of unreality) (*GW 17*, p. 1007) then he should have realized that, in proffering a recognizably *real* moral, he was going counter to his own demands. There may be an operatic solution to the problem of developing *das Lehrhafte* (the didactic) from *das Kulinarische* (the culinary), but the way would appear to lie along the paths of Rossini and Donizetti, or—even more likely—in the works of Mozart, a possibility which Brecht tacitly acknowledges by referring to *Zauberflöte* and *Figaro* with approval for their 'aktivistische Elemente' (activist elements) (*GW 17*, p. 1013).

The Marxist Plays

If *Mahagonny* displays a slightly uneasy combination of *das Lehrhafte* and *das Kulinarische*, the other works Brecht was working on at the time sacrifice much of the latter to the de-demands of the former. These are the *Lehrstücke*, the didactic plays which begin with *Der Flug der Lindberghs* (The Flight of the Lindberghs) and end with *Die Horatier und die Kuriatier* (The Horatii and the Curiatii). Their purpose is avowedly didactic and political, and while *Mahagonny* is Marxist by implication, these works are for the most part examinations of the principles of Marxism as well as formal illustrations of a dialectical view of the world and of society. Brecht's initial view—which he later came to modify—was that the *Lehrstück* teaches by virtue of its being performed, *not* by virtue of its being watched by an audience. This is an admittedly extreme standpoint, and one that holds true more for *Der Jasager* and *Der Neinsager* and *Die Massnahme* than for *Die Ausnahme und die Regel*. Taken to its logical conclusion, such a philosophy would involve the total exclusion of an audience: the actors are the only ones to derive any benefit from a performance. But if the audience is not to be taught, why bother to use the stage at all? The plays could just as well be staged in the spartan comfort of a worker's living-room, thus providing a proletarian equivalent to the bourgeois soirées of *Hausmusik* (music in the home) that were once so popular. Brecht must have realized the shortcomings of this quasi-élitist view of the ideal audience, because he immediately qualifies and balances his initial extreme position by stating that the audience can of course be 'utilized', even though its presence is essentially unnecessary—

which sounds rather like a case of wanting to eat your cake and have it as well.

In the *Lehrstück*, with all its positive Marxist didactic elements, it would be wrong to imagine that *only* socially positive and commendable actions are to be presented. Even from the depiction of the most blatantly asocial actions and attitudes, some educational effect can be gained. The simple and uncomplicated plot is intended to provide an easily manageable framework for the political moral, and both the language and the characterization are reduced to the bare essentials. Strikingly individual or idiosyncratic characters are either completely absent or are made use of only because the individual or unique aspect of their attitude or actions is to be the subject of the lesson. Yet it would be wrong to see these plays, for all their formal austerity and bleakness, as mere drum-beating, unimaginative propaganda. Brecht's use of dialectics, as a method both of argument and construction, ensures that all sides of a particular problem are subjected to scrutiny. The audience is not browbeaten into accepting uncritically the author's standpoint: rather are they presented with an examination of a set of circumstances which is intended to encourage them to arrive at a rational decision in favour of the Marxist message.

The plays are in effect illustrations of Brecht's own conception of the learning process. They are not flat replicas of a classroom scene with the teacher haranguing his class with a raised forefinger, but stage equivalents of a Platonic or Socratic school, in which the teacher is an equal partner with the pupils in the discussion. Brecht himself always viewed learning as a *process* involving the audience, the play, the actors and the playwright. The criticism of the didactic elements he dismissed out of hand, saying,

> Es ist also jetzt nicht mehr die Frage: Soll gelehrt werden?
> Es ist jetzt die Frage: Wie soll gelehrt und gelernt werden?[1]
>
> (*GW 17*, p. 1027)

It is typical of his procedure that the question of method as-

[1] It is then no longer a question of: should there be any teaching? The question is now: what form should the teaching and learning take?

sumes paramount importance. And if this were to prove sterile
and unproductive, the resulting plays would merit little attention. But Brecht's use of the techniques of his 'epic' theatre in
works like *Die Massnahme* (The Measures Taken) and *Die
Ausnahme und die Regel* is a triumphant vindication of his
method.

Even allowing for the two-dimensional character presentation and the flat, colourless language, these plays are remarkably
successful in theatrical terms. So much so that the reader who
decides in advance that they are Communist primers for tiny
tots comes to recognize that the flatness of the written word
becomes an essential theatrical ingredient. It gives the works
something of the powerful immediacy of a ritual in which
tribal and social elements join hands: tribal, in that the characters' emotions are heavily stylized; social, in that the characters are seen as representatives of a particular class. The role
of the merchant in *Die Ausnahme und die Regel* shows how
much Brecht can make of such a character. His opening address to the audience sets out both his character and the motives
for his present and subsequent behaviour:

> Ich bin der Kaufmann Karl Langmann und reise nach
> Urga, um die Schlussverhandlungen über eine Konzession
> zu führen. Hinter mir her kommen die Konkurrenten.
> Wer zuerst ankommt, macht das Geschäft. Durch meine
> Schlauheit und meine Energie bei der Überwindung aller
> Schwierigkeiten und meiner Unerbittlichkeit gegen mein
> Personal habe ich die Reise bisher beinahe in der Hälfte
> der üblichen Zeit gemacht.[1]   (*GW 2*, p. 795)

Throughout the work, this emphasis on 'the survival of the
fittest' as the only way of existing is repeated, and, since the
law is 'an eye for an eye', he is finally acquitted of the coolie's
murder. Given the situation in which exploitation is expected,

---

[1] I am the merchant Karl Langmann and I am travelling to Urga to
conduct the final negotiations for a concession. Behind me come my com-
petitors. He who arrives first gets the business. By my cunning and my
energy in the surmounting of all difficulties and my unrelenting attitude
towards my employees I have made the journey thus far in almost half the
usual time.

given the relationship between master and servant, given, in
short, the law of the jungle, the court makes the right decision
in acquitting the merchant. But it is a decision of relative
justice only: the audience must then consider the injustice of
such a 'correct' judgement and provide a remedy. Or, as Brecht
was later to write in a poem addressed to Danish actors:

> . . . Und da könnt ihr Schauspieler der Arbeiter, lern-
> end und lehrend
> Mit eurer Gestaltung eingreifen in alle Kämpfe
> Vom Menschen eurer Zeit und so
> Mit dem Ernst des Studiums und der Heiterkeit des
> Wissens
> Helfen, die Erfahrung des Kampfs zum Gemeingut zu
> machen und
> Die Gerechtigkeit zur Leidenschaft.[1]
>
> (*GW 9*, pp. 765–6)

That the techniques of the epic theatre—its bareness, its lack
of colour in both set and language, its direct addresses to the
audience, its narrative rather than dramatic style—could be
successful when used in a full-scale work, is shown by *Die
Mutter* (The Mother). It is the best example in Brecht's work
of the most literal application of the techniques of epic theatre
allied with an uncompromisingly direct dose of Marxism. In a
sequence of fourteen scenes spanning the years 1905–17 Brecht
shows the transformation of Pelagea Wlassowa from an un-
political worker's wife into a militant supporter of the Revolution. Where initially she passively grieves over the fact that
she cannot give her son enough food, she comes to realize in
the course of the play that this passivity changes nothing, and
that active involvement in the revolutionary process is necessary. When her son Pavel is arrested, she decides to distribute
the pamphlets in the factory; and from this moment on, she

---

[1] . . . And that is where you, the workers' actors, learning and teaching
With your presentation can take a hand in all the struggles
Of men of your time, and thereby
With the seriousness of study and the cheerfulness of knowledge
Help to turn the experience of the struggle into common property and
To turn justice into a passion.

becomes more and more committed to the struggle against authority and oppression.

The work's simplicity of structure and content is deceptive: Pelagea Wlassowa is no naïve peasant who suddenly experiences an apocalyptic revelation of the true nature of Communism and goes forth like a Socialist St Joan to win back the world for the workers. She is a reasonable, down-to-earth realist who, facing up to the wrongs and injustices of the situation, makes a logical decision in favour of Communism. At the same time, she is far from being a cool-headed, unfeeling and all too rational puppet in the hands of her Marxist master. She possesses common sense without smugness, native cunning without artful intrigue, a spontaneity free of false enthusiasm. She has much in common with Mutter Courage, though she is a more 'positive' heroine: yet even now she (unjustifiably) stands in the latter's shadow. It is no accident that Brecht's *Arbeitsjournal* (work-journal) has Margarete Steffin singling out Pelagea Wlassowa as the character dearest to her. Brecht shows her in a variety of situations: anxious that she has too little soup for her son, receiving a lesson in the elementary economics of existence, bringing home to a woman the injustice of her situation shortly after she has received the news of her son's death. Her grief is moving without becoming sentimental, her defence of Communism direct and persuasive, free of that embarrassing artlessness which is so often found in such characters. The last lines of the 'Lob des Kommunismus' (In Praise of Communism) present *in nuce* not only the essence of the argument, they provide an accurate description of the skill needed to create both Wlassowa and a play like *Die Mutter*:

> Es ist das Einfache
> Das schwer zu machen ist.[1]
>
> <div align="right">(<i>GW 2</i>, p. 852)</div>

---

[1] It is simplicity itself
Difficult only in the realization.

4

The Exceptional Individual

After *Die Mutter*, Brecht's dramas show a movement away from such extreme austerity towards the development of a richer dramatic style and a rounded, often more ambivalent presentation of character. The economy of means and directness of expression acquired during the work on the *Lehrstücke* and *Die Mutter* are retained, and to them is added an interest in a more subtle use of language as a means of character-presentation. Brecht's gifts as a writer were essentially those of the poet, rather than the dramatist: whether it be the effusive, deliberately extravagant lyricism of *Baal*, the sober, factual testimony of *Die Ausnahme und die Regel* or the often wordy exchanges of *Leben des Galilei*, so dense with rhetoric and metaphor, Brecht's language is never unwieldy or bloodless. If one looks for a common denominator in the mature dramas, it is to be found in this distinctive language and in certain recurrent themes. For, in terms of structure and dramatic style, the dramas display an astonishing variety. In 1941 Brecht himself noted, not without a hint of uneasiness:

> wenn ich meine letzten stücke betrachte und vergleiche, *Galilei, Mutter Courage, Furcht und Elend, Der gute Mensch von Sezuan, Herr Puntila und sein Knecht Matti, Aufstieg des Ui,* so finde ich sie abnorm uneinheitlich in jeder weise, selbst die genres wechseln unaufhörlich. biographie, gestarium, parabel, charakterlustspiel im volkston, historienfarce—die stücke streben auseinander wie die gestirne im neuen weltbild der physik, als sei auch hier irgendein kern der dramatik explodiert.[1]

(*AJ*, p. 274)

[1] when i look at my latest plays and compare them—*Galilei, Mother Courage, Fear and Misery, The Good Person of Szechwan, Mr Puntila and*

For all this, however, *Galilei, Mutter Courage* and *Der gute Mensch* have much in common, in terms of their themes and the presentation of character. Each portrays the exceptional individual, in turn at odds with, or endeavouring to profit from the situation in which he or she is set. And in each case, the setting of the play does have, if not in every case a parabolic, then at least a symbolic function. Galileo's Italy is not merely Renaissance Italy: it is also a model for a society in which the individual must decide whether he can afford to be a hero or not. Courage's Europe of the Thirty Years' War is both that *and* the Europe of the third decade of the twentieth century, as well as a model for an extreme situation in which the individual fights to exist with every means at his disposal. Shen Te's Sezuan is to be found in Brecht's own fictional China, where a jarring combination of East and West is more important than realism or verisimilitude. In such a country the author can with impunity introduce Oriental atmosphere, three Gods and a pilot, a water-carrier and a baker, and a kind-hearted prostitute who assumes her cousin's identity and a disguise that would fool nobody. Sezuan, as Brecht explicitly indicates, *does* have a parabolical purpose. It is a model of the world in which the exploited suffer not only at the hands of the exploiters but also at the hands of their fellows: where to exist, the individual, instead of bestowing charity, must resort to the same methods that others practise. *Galileo* is the most reflective and discursive of the three, and the most conventional in terms of its structure. In *Mutter Courage* there is more dramatic action, more excitement and more extremes of emotions, while *Der gute Mensch* best displays Brecht's lyrical gifts as well as his enduring fondness for the *Schaubuden-Theater* (fairground theatre). The play is a montage of various theatrical styles,

---

his servant Matti, The Rise of Ui—i find them terribly heterogeneous in every respect, even the genres change incessantly, biography, gestarium, parable, character-comedy in the popular vein, history-farce—the plays spin away from one another like the stars in the new cosmology of physics, as if here too some nucleus of the dramatic art is exploding.

(Throughout the *Arbeitsjournal* Brecht discards the German convention of using capital letters for nouns: in the English translations this characteristic has been retained.)

drawing on the Noh Theatre, the morality play, traditional puppet plays and cabaret-type sketches and songs.

Leben des Galilei (Galileo)

Though in *Die Mutter* Brecht had already written a play round a dominating central figure, the scale and concept of *Leben des Galilei* were larger than anything he had so far attempted. The play follows the course of Galileo's career from 1609–42: the scenes follow in chronological order, but the aim is not a complete biographical portrait of Galileo. Sometimes a few days separate the scenes, at other times several years. In the opening scenes we watch Galileo pursuing his researches, tricking the authorities into accepting the telescope as his own invention and deciding to move from Venice to Florence in the search for congenial surroundings and, above all, patronage. But he finds himself isolated, his discoveries largely ignored and denounced by the Inquisition. He is forced to suspend his investigations into the planets as these are throwing doubt on the entire Ptolemaic system and, by extension, on the accepted ordered and hierarchical view of cosmology and society. When a new pope is elected who had previously been sympathetic towards his views, Galileo is encouraged to resume his researches. But his hopes for the dissemination of his theories are short-lived: he is summoned before the Inquisition and forced to recant. He remains a prisoner of the Inquisition for the rest of his life; and when his former pupil Andrea calls on him he gives him the *Discorsi* to smuggle out of Italy and at the same time condemns himself for his cowardice and his betrayal of science.

Described as 'a dramatic biography' the play also originally carried the title *Die Erde bewegt sich* (The Earth moves) a title which reads more like an attempt to popularize and sell the story of Galileo. However, the first mention of the play in the *Arbeitsjournal* is as *Das Leben des Galilei*. There are a number of interesting observations concerning the work's origins which can be drawn from this title and from Brecht's discussions at the time with his friend Ferdinand Reyher, who had connections with the Hollywood film industry and who visited

Brecht in Denmark in 1938. From a letter to Reyher, it is clear that the two of them had been discussing a plan for a *film* rather than a play on the subject of Galileo. This, and Brecht's own enduring interest in the cinema throughout his life, account for a number of elements in the play which have hitherto received little attention.

The choice of the figure of Galileo is the first of these. Previously, all Brecht's full-length dramas had been set in either the present (clearly defined, as in *Furcht und Elend des Dritten Reiches* (Terror and Misery of the Third Reich), or less clearly, as in *Mann ist Mann*) or the immediate past. Why then this move back to Renaissance Italy? Obviously, the topical aspect of the Galileo theme appealed; but even more obviously, the choice of this period and the creation of such a role were prompted by commercial thoughts. The thirties saw a whole spate of films presenting the lives of famous figures in history, the most famous being *The Story of Louis Pasteur*, *The Life of Emile Zola*, *Rembrandt* and (possibly the best-known) *The Private Life of Henry VIII*. It now seems much more than a coincidence that Charles Laughton appeared in the last two, especially since the Brecht–Laughton collaboration was later to prove so productive for the second version of *Leben des Galilei*. The part of Galileo could, even from the beginning, have been written with Laughton in mind. Brecht knew and admired Laughton's films, especially *The Private Life of Henry VIII* (he was later to suggest the title *The Private Life of the Master Race* for his own *Furcht und Elend des Dritten Reiches*) and there is little doubt that he was partly prompted to write what he called a *Riesenrolle* (star part) by what he took to be the state of the film market at the time. Indeed, the more one looks at the character of Galileo in the fourteenth scene (his failing physical condition coupled with his still avid interest in food, the relationship with his daughter and the way she treats him), the more one is reminded of Laughton's performance as the ageing king, with unaffected appetite, left to the care of his sixth wife, Catherine Parr.

The two sides of Galileo's character are fixed by the very first words he addresses to Andrea: 'Stell die Milch auf den

Tisch, aber klapp kein Buch zu.' (Put the milk on the table, but shut none of the books). The sensualist and the scientist, the *bon-vivant* and the seeker after truth, the man for whom an old wine is as important as a new idea—these are the apparently contradictory qualities in the character of Galileo. Apparently contradictory because both for the character and the author they are really part of the same basic impulse. The urge that drives Galileo to seek to extend the boundaries of science is the self-same urge that drives him to seek the physical comforts he desires. As he says to Sagredo: 'Mein Lieber, ich brauche Musse. Ich brauche Beweise. Und ich will die Fleischtöpfe' (My dear fellow, I need leisure. I need proofs. And I want the flesh-pots) (*GW 3*, p. 1259). The self-centred tone of such pronouncements hints at Galileo's own egotism: he is self-sufficient, greedy for the truth, and tends towards a dogmatism in the *tone* of his pronouncements which is often at odds with the attitude they profess. This opposition is effectively realized in the rhetorical devices Brecht employs in the dialogue and the lengthy monologues that Galileo delivers. Throughout the play, Brecht's interest in structural and thematic balance and contrast—which goes hand in hand with his dialectical argumentation—is reflected not only in the structure of individual scenes and their relationship to each other, but in the very language itself.

Galileo's opening discourse—which Brecht aptly described as an aria—bristles with antithesis and parallelism, and with conventional, though marvellously poised rhetoric, heightened by vivid and effective imagery:

> Denn die alte Zeit ist herum, und es ist eine neue Zeit . . .
> Die Städte sind eng und so sind die Köpfe. Aberglauben
> und Pest. Aber jetzt heisst es: da es so ist, bleibt es nicht
> so. Denn alles bewegt sich, mein Freund. Ich denke gerne,
> dass es mit den Schiffen anfing. Seit Menschengedenken
> waren sie nur an den Küsten entlang gekrochen, aber
> plötzlich verliessen sie die Küsten und liefen aus über alle
> Meere.[1]   (*GW 3*, p. 1232–3)

[1] For the old times are past and this is a new age . . . the cities are narrow, and peoples' minds with them. Superstition and plague. But

The fondness for such images is an essential trait in Galileo's character, as well as in his creator's. Though he advances arguments and postulates theories in the course of the play, it is never in a dull or academically dry language. His speech is the speech of a scientist who loves words as much as he loves his science; so much so that at times he even *thinks* in images. The idea of seeking new horizons contained in the final sentence above is re-stated in similar terms throughout the play: e.g.

> . . . selbst im Schachspiel die Türme gehen neuerdings weit über alle Felder;[1] (ibid., p. 1234)

> Jetzt spielt man doch so, dass die grösseren Figuren über alle Felder gehen . . . Nicht an den Küsten lang, einmal muss man ausfahren.[2] (ibid., p. 1284–5)

Given the aptness and directness of such illustrations, it is no surprise that Galileo has little patience with those who cannot grasp their wider implications. Because of his belief in the power of reason and in man as a rational being, he cannot calmly accept the irrational behaviour of those who do not share his views and thereby deny the evidence of their own eyes. In this connection, two of Galileo's own remarks are worth noting. Although he elsewhere shows that he is well aware of the possible wider implications of his investigations, he does not set out to erect a scientific and philosophical system for which every conceivable grandiose claim can be made. In his own words:

> Eine Hauptursache der Armut in den Wissenschaften ist meist eingebildeter Reichtum. Es ist nicht ihr Ziel, der

---

now we say: just because things are thus and thus, they don't stay that way. Because, my friend, everything is in motion. I like to think that the ships started it all. From time immemorial they had hugged the coastline, but suddenly they left the coastline and sailed forth over the oceans.

[1] . . . recently, even in chess the rooks range widely over every field.

[2] But now it's played in such a way that the larger pieces can range over every field . . . Not creeping along the coastline, you've got to venture forth one day.

unendlichen Weisheit eine Tür zu öffnen, sondern eine
Grenze zu setzen dem unendlichen Irrtum.[1]

(*GW 3*, p. 1304)

(It is relevant to note that the above quotation echoes a remark
of Francis Bacon's, to be found in his 'Preface to the Great
Instauration':

> ... nor to imagine that this Instauration of mine is a
> thing infinite and beyond the power of man, when it is in
> fact the true end and termination of infinite error.)

And later in the same scene, he makes a further defence of his
approach to scientific investigation:

> Meine Absicht ist nicht, zu beweisen, dass ich bisher recht
> gehabt habe, sondern: herauszufinden, ob. Ich sage: lasst
> alle Hoffnung fahren, ihr, die ihr in die Beobachtung
> eintretet.[2]   (*GW 3*, p. 1311)

It is a good instance of Brecht's use of phraseology drawn from
various areas: the antithetical layout of the first sentence, the
quasi-bliblical 'Ich sage', the parodying of Dante's 'lasciate
ogni speranza voi ch'entrate'. And determining the attitude the
lines express is an empirical approach to scientific problems,
as well as a healthy doubting of discoveries already made,
which is in the same vein as Bacon's

> If a man will begin with certainties, he shall end in doubts;
> but if he will be content to begin with doubts, he shall end
> in certainties.

So far, only Galileo's attitudes towards scientific discovery
have been considered. But for Brecht there is another question,
which assumes increasing importance through the three versions
of the play—namely, the social responsibility of the scientist.
To what extent can and should the scientist concern himself

---

[1] One main reason for the poverty of science is usually its imagined
richness. Its goal is not to open the gateway to everlasting wisdom, but to
set a limit to everlasting error.

[2] My aim is not to prove that up till now I've been right but to find out
whether or not I *have* been. What I say is: abandon hope, all ye who enter
upon observation.

with the possible application and effect of his researches? Brecht the Marxist was more concerned with this problem than Galileo. The latter, though he indicates at various times during the play (especially in Scene 9) that his discoveries have a significance outside the purely scientific, also professes a lack of concern for the consequences of his work:

> Ich würde meinen, als Wissenschaftler haben wir uns nicht zu fragen, wohin die Wahrheit uns führen mag.[1]
>
> (*GW 3*, p. 1270)

> Ich habe ein Buch geschrieben über die Mechanik des Universums, das ist alles. Was daraus gemacht oder nicht gemacht wird, geht mich nichts an.[2]
>
> (*GW 3*, p. 1319)

Such remarks help to reinforce the more negative view of Galileo's character that Brecht arrived at during his work on the three versions of the play. For one of Brecht's main arguments, which he puts into the mouth of Galileo in Scene 14, is that the scientist *cannot* afford to be indifferent to the use to which his discoveries are put. Had he not recanted, Galileo goes on—and even in the final version of the play it is the author rather than the character who is speaking—something akin to a Hippocratic oath for scientists could have been formulated.

It is hard to accept the feasibility of this suggestion. As Eric Bentley puts it:

> To condemn Galileo for his abjuration, one must believe, first that he had a real alternative and, second, that this alternative was worth all the trouble.

Giordano Bruno had not recanted and had been burnt at the stake. Is there any evidence—apart from the words Brecht gives his own character—to suppose that Galileo would have escaped a similar fate? Again, in Bentley's words, '. . . there

---

[1] I submit that as scientists we have no business asking where the truth may lead us.

[2] I have written a book about the mechanism of the universe, that's all. What people make or don't make of it is no concern of mine.

is something absurd in asking Galileo Galilei to strike a blow for the philosophy of Bertolt Brecht.' And if one takes Brecht's argument to its logical conclusion, one is entitled to ask why he did not write a drama about a figure who remained true to his principles and provided a positive example for posterity. The answer is simple: noble heroes, even those with a well-developed social conscience, nowadays make for dull drama— witness Morris West's attempt to treat the fate and character of Giordano Bruno. The Galileo who recanted may well merit Brecht's criticism. Yet he is still a far more complex and riveting character; and the questions raised by Brecht's drama (even if they provoke an apologia for the character rather than the desired rejection) can only be raised by a work in which the central figure does in fact display what Bentley calls 'a certain kind of weakness'. For all that it breaks with the traditional view of character in German drama, Brecht's *Leben des Galilei* has one thing in common with the idealistic dramas of Schiller, Kleist and even Hebbel. In their works, the individual fails but the idea prevails: in Brecht, while the individual likewise fails, it is dialectics that is *intended* to prevail as the means of coming to terms both with the world of the play and with society in general.

Mutter Courage und ihre Kinder (Mother Courage and Her Children)

In one of his numerous notes on the character of Galileo, Brecht, speaking of the fourteenth scene, writes:

> In der kalifornischen Fassung . . . bricht Galileo die Lobeshymnen seines Schülers ab und beweist ihm, dass der Widerruf ein Verbrechen war und durch das Werk, so wichtig es sein mochte, nicht aufgewogen. Wenn es jemanden interessieren sollte: Dies ist auch das Urteil des Stückeschriebers.[1]   (*GW 17*, p. 1133)

[1] In the Californian version Galileo cuts off his pupil's eulogies and proves to him that the recantation was a crime and not made up for by the results of his work, no matter how important they may be. If anyone is interested: this is also the playwright's judgement.

It is a rather diffident and off-hand way of passing judgement on the character, and more in keeping with an attitude towards Galileo which does not exclusively praise or condemn, but contains praise and rejection of his actions. Brecht's comments on the character of Mutter Courage tend, however, to be more negative—so much so, that at times it appears that he is being deliberately perverse. For Brecht's presentation of her character is just as dialectical as in the case of Galileo. Where the latter's scientific zeal and zest for living both spring from the same basic impulse, the character of Courage is brought to life by the tragic contradiction between mother and tradeswoman. She sets out to profit from the war, because she sees this as the only adequate means of ensuring the survival of herself and her family; and the play's title indicates the importance of the children to the play.

It is not merely a play about Courage, but about Courage *and* her children; if they occupy a secondary place beside her (in terms of their characterization) what happens to them is of greater importance for the action than what happens to Courage herself. With her wagon and her three children she follows in the tracks of the armies involved in the Thirty Years' War. She loses her elder son Eilif to the recruiting officers in the play's opening scene, and this loss is an ominous anticipation of what is to follow. Five years later her other son, Schweizerkas, now paymaster of a Protestant regiment, is captured by the Catholics: she effectively sentences him to death because she haggles too long over the price of his freedom. Eilif's boldness, which had sustained him in the war, proves his downfall during a time of peace: he is executed for a deed which in war-time would have gained him honour and commendation. Courage herself loses the opportunity to opt out of the war when she turns down Pfeifenpieter's offer to go with him: she stays with her wagon and Kattrin, only to lose her when, in an attempt to warn a town of an imminent attack, she is shot down by the imperial troops. We are left with the bleak picture of Courage still following the armies in the hope that she will find Eilif—whom she still imagines to be alive. For her, the course of the war is the course of the life and death of her children. The mighty historical events have their counterpart in this account of the annihilation of a family, for within this circle Brecht presents a microcosm of the world outside.

Courage is in turn admirable and despicable, her instinct for survival forcing her at one moment to suppress her emotion when confronted with Schweizerkas's corpse, and the next, leading to her callousness towards her daughter and the wounded soldiers at Magdeburg. In her, there are more extreme traits of character than in Galileo, her emotions and reactions provoke—whether Brecht likes it or not—a more direct response from the audience. Yet this should not mean that the audience *throughout* uncritically identifies with Courage. The understanding of her behaviour does not necessarily involve bestowing on each action the stamp of approval. She is cunning, avaricious and selfish: yet she is also warm, vital and endowed with a keen sense of humour. Her cunning is but the other side of her quick wit; her avarice a negative form of a necessary and shrewd business sense; and her warmth, vitality and humour are her means of survival. In the course of the play, Brecht introduces moments where he tries to make clear that Courage could have opted out of the war. But does she in fact have any choice? In the very first scene, in reply to the *Feldwebel*'s (sergeant) question about the reason for her name, she makes two remarks that provide important clues to her character:

> Courage heiss ich, weil ich den Ruin gefürchtet hab, Feldwebel, und bin durch das Geschützfeuer von Riga gefahrn mit fünfzig Brotlaib im Wagen. Sie waren schon angeschimmelt, es war höchste Zeit, ich hab keine Wahl gehabt.[1]　　　　　　　　　　　(*GW 4*, p. 1351)

The humorous paradoxical combination of 'Courage' and 'Ruin' is equivalent to the larger and tragic paradox of Courage's own predicament. And her final words, though they apply to this particular incident, invite a wider application—the

[1] I'm called Courage because I was afraid of being ruined, sergeant, and drove through the cannon fire round Riga with fifty loaves of bread in the wagon. They were already mouldy, it was high time to get rid of them, I had no choice.

battle round Riga left her no choice, does not the Thirty Years' War itself similarly leave her no real choice? War makes its own rules, and survival at such times tends to depend on a manipulation of these rules.

It is all very well for Brecht to observe that 'who sups with the devil needs a long spoon'—the truth of that and the *Feldwebel*'s 'Will vom Krieg leben/Wird ihm wohl müssen auch was geben' (Want to live off the war,/You'll have to give it something to even the score) (*GW 4*, p. 1360) is not disputed. But the play itself also makes brutally clear—notably in 'Das Lied von der grossen Kapitulation' (The song of the great capitulation) and the 'Salomonsong'—that ordinary virtues are not only meaningless, but even dangerous in war. This is not the same as saying that war is inevitable, that one should accept the situation, and merely wonder at the blind tenacity of Courage. An entry from the *Arbeitsjournal* shows the author's own awareness of the way war nullifies all accepted patterns of behaviour:

> die *Mutter Courage* durchstudierend, sehe ich mit einiger zufriedenheit, wie der krieg als riesiges feld ercheint, nicht unähnlich den feldern der neuen physik, in denen die körper merkwürdige abweichungen erfahren. alle berechnungsarten des individuums, gezogen aus erfahrungen des friedens, versagen; es geht nicht mit kühnheit, es geht nicht mit vorsicht, nicht mit ehrlichkeit, nicht mit betrug, nicht mit brutalität noch mit mitleid, alles bringt untergang. aber es bleiben die kräfte, welche auch den frieden zu einem krieg machten, die unnennbaren.[1]
>
> (*AJ*, p. 221)

The play both condemns the weakness and recognizes the strength of Courage: Brecht condemns her, more harshly than the audience, for what she *does*, while the audience cannot suppress a sneaking admiration for what she *is*—the embodi-

---

[1] going through *Mother Courage* i note with some satisfaction how the war appears like an enormous field, not unlike the fields of modern physics in which bodies undergo peculiar deviations. every method of calculation at an individual's disposal which is drawn from experiences of peace fails; boldness is no good, caution is no good, honesty is no good, trickery is no good, nor brutality, nor sympathy, everything brings destruction. but there remain the forces that turn even peace into war—the unmentionable ones.

ment of the survival instinct. The Zurich audience in 1941 may have come away with only sympathy for Courage the mother, who, like Niobe, sees her children destroyed by more powerful forces but struggles on regardless. But to see the play solely in these terms is to turn a blind eye to at least half the text, and involves a complete disregard for Brecht's methods of characterization. Admittedly, he invites this danger by choosing an archetypal Niobe-figure as his central character. But he adds negative elements to this character, sets her in a completely different set of surroundings and invites the audience to consider these as well. A further diary entry has some bearing on this problem. In 1940 he had coined a new quasi-technical expression 'titularium', used for the collective description and summarizing of stages in the action of a particular scene and aspects of character:

> bei dem aufstellen des titulariums zu *Courage* wird alles psychologische völlig vernachlässigt. sogar der plot wird kaum berücksichtigt (die niobehandlung). ganz zu schweigen vom zeitkolorit.[1] (*AJ*, p. 214)

Particularly revealing is the implied awareness of elements in the play which are omitted from this 'titularium'—which is not at all the same as saying that Brecht's relationship to his work was schizophrenic or that he was intent on suppressing 'recognizable human qualities'. What is evident here is the playwright's search for a method of *Umfunktionierung* (finding a new function)—setting an old myth in a new situation in such a way that this will also receive its due weight and attention.

The difficulty is, however, that the audience will fasten on to what is recognizable and familiar—precisely because of the author's gift for characterization—so that they neglect the other aspects, or else notice them only out of the corner of their eye. This is precisely what occurs in the final scene of the play. One realizes that Courage is blind, that she has learnt

[1] in drawing up the 'chapter headings' for *Courage* all psychological elements are completely disregarded. even the plot is hardly taken into account (the niobe-action). not to mention the mood of the times.

nothing, that it is now up to the audience to learn from what they have observed—and then Brecht, with one stroke, spoils it all, at least in his own terms. Who is left on the stage at the end? Courage, who, hitching herself once more to the wagon, struggles off after the soldiers. In closing the play on this scene, Brecht is making use of one of the oldest 'tear-jerking' devices of the silent cinema, and in particular of the films of Chaplin—the walk-off. Just like Chaplin's tramp, Brecht's Courage, at this moment above all others, represents and drives home the pathos of the human situation. It is not so much that she is a symbol of indestructibility, but rather that she *has been destroyed* by what has taken place and yet, blind to the realities, still insists on hoping against hope. Or, as the final screen caption to *Modern Times* puts it: 'Don't buck. Never say die.' One of Brecht's notes on Weigel's performance as Courage comes closest to her tragic predicament as well as showing that the historical and, by extension, social situation is responsible for her attitudes and cries out for change:

> Die dem Pulikum tief fühlbare Tragik der Courage und ihres Lebens bestand darin, dass hier ein entsetzlicher Widerspruch bestand, der einen Menschen vernichtete, ein Widerspruch, der gelöst werden konnte, aber nur von der Gesellschaft selbst und in langen, schrecklichen Kämpfen. Und die sittliche Überlegenheit dieser Art der Darstellung bestand darin, dass der Mensch als zerstörbar gezeigt wurde, selbst der lebenskräftigste![1]
>
> (*GW 16*, p. 896)

Der gute Mensch von Sezuan (The Good Person of Szechwan)

Where Courage is concerned with the difficulty of living and profiting from living, Shen Te in *Der gute Mensch von Sezuan*

[1] The tragedy of *Mother Courage* and of her life, which the audience could feel deeply, lay in the fact that here was a terrible contradiction which destroyed a human being, a contradiction which could be resolved, but only by society itself in the course of long, terrible struggles. And the moral superiority of this way of playing the part lay in the fact that the human being—even the most vital individual—was shown to be destructible.

is concerned with what appears to be a more idealistic problem. Addressing the gods at the end of the play, she says:

> Euer einstiger Befehl
> Gut zu sein und doch zu leben
> Zerriss mich wie ein Blitz in zwei Hälften.[1]
>
> (*GW 4*, p. 1603)

Although Brecht succeeds in providing a framework of convincing social questions and situations, the fact remains that the question 'how to live and yet be good' can be seen equally well as a metaphysical problem. It has certainly been the subject of investigations by most philosophers of ethics since Aristotle. Yet the world of this play is a long way from the ordered optimism of Pope's lines in the Third Epistle of his *Essay on Man*:

> Thus God and Nature linked the general frame,
> And bade Self-Love and Social be the same.

The twentieth-century Marxist can only dismiss the comfortable harmony of this piece of mysticism, masquerading as common sense; in its place he sets a view of life and society where 'Self-Love' and 'Social' must inevitably be at odds with each other. Accordingly, Brecht underlines the conflict, at the same time giving it dramatic point and impact, by dividing his central character into the 'good' Shen Te and the 'evil' Shui Ta. When Shen Te's distribution of charity seems likely to bring about her own ruin, she dons the disguise of Shui Ta, with the intention of 'being cruel to be kind'. In introducing such a *physical* manifestation of emotional and/or psychological urges and of contradictory personality traits, Brecht seeks to avoid the dangers of a *purely* psychological or *purely* deterministic view of character.

Compared with both *Leben des Galilei* and *Mutter Courage und ihre Kinder*, *Der gute Mensch von Sezuan* is a play whose structure, loose even by Brecht's standards, suffers from a certain unwieldiness, while the plot, because of its essentially

---

[1]   Your earlier command
To be good and yet to live
Tore me in two like a bolt of lightning.

schematic nature, sometimes appears sketchy and at times contrived. Three gods arrive in Sezuan seeking both lodgings and one good human being. But in this city even the poor are indifferent. The prostitute Shen Te who finally gives them shelter is rewarded—though only because she requests it—with a small amount of money which she uses to set up a small tobacco shop.

This comparative wealth immediately makes her the prey both of parasites and those less fortunate, and she is soon on the brink of financial disaster. Forced to assume the identity of her 'evil' cousin Shui Ta, she succeeds in preventing herself from going under, but at the cost of the loss of her self-esteem and her previously happy relationships with those around her. When Shen Te eventually 'returns', she falls in love with the out-of-work flyer Sun, who, however, takes advantage both of her devotion and her money. He is on the point of leaving her pregnant for a job in Peking when Shui Ta 'reappears' again, sets up a tobacco factory and forces all those whom Shen-Te helped to work for him for low wages. The business thrives, but when the townspeople become suspicious about Shen Te's absence and suspect Shui Ta of murdering her, he is summoned before the court. Shui Ta is 'unmasked' in the presence of the three gods who decline to give any answer to Shen Te's complaints and questions and return to their heavenly domain mouthing lofty thoughts and leaving her in the same predicament as before. Their one generous concession is the condoning of the occasional 'use' of the evil Shui Ta.

Brecht had more difficulties with this play than with any other of his dramas. The motif of the prostitute disguised as a man dates from 1927, while an idea for a play *Die Ware Liebe* (an untranslatable pun—'love for sale/true love') was noted in 1930 and he had often during the intervening decade attempted to work it into shape. And the motif of the gods arriving unheralded in a town, and being finally recognized by one inhabitant, is based on an incident described in the poem 'Matinée in Dresden'. (Brecht, Döblin and Arnolt Bronnen had arrived to attend the première of a work by Franz Werfel, only to find themselves out in the cold.)

Even in the work as it now stands, it is impossible to over-look resultant weaknesses that Brecht himself, with his custom-ary critical eye, noted in 1940:

> li gung [who later became shen te] musste ein mensch sein, damit sie ein guter mensch sein konnte. sie ist also nicht stereotyp gut, ganz gut, in jedem augenblick gut, auch als li gung nicht. und lao go ist nicht stereotyp bös usw. das ineinanderübergehen der beiden figuren, ihr ständiger zerfall usw. scheint nur halbwegs gelungen, das grosse experiment der götter, dem gebot der nächstenliebe das gebot der selbstliebe hinzuzufügen, dem >du sollst zu andern gut sein< das >du sollst zu dir selbst gut sein< musste sich zugleich abheben von der fabel und sie doch beherrschen. die moralischen prästationen mussten sozial motiviert sein. jedoch mussten sie auch einem besonderen vermögen (besonderen talent, besonderer veranlagung) zugeschrieben werden.[1]   (*AJ*, p. 116)

Yet, perhaps because the play, of all the mature dramas, pays least attention to the idea of 'the well-made play', because Brecht packs the scenes with so many contrasting levels of style and emotion, the work retains a freshness which one misses occasionally in *Mutter Courage*, more frequently in *Leben des Galilei*. The work lacks the dense yet pointed argumentation of *Leben des Galilei*, has neither the depth nor the impact of *Mutter Courage*. Yet it makes up for these de-ficiencies with its poetic language, its colourful minor charac-ters and its structure which, while apparently cumbersome, can, in performance, combine exuberance and liveliness with a resonant stillness.

Essentially the work is a modern parable-masque: Brecht uses characters who can be seen as descendants of traditional

[1] li gung [who later became shen te] had to be a person in order to be a good person. she is, then, not the stereotype of goodness, totally good, good at every moment, not even as li gung; and lao go is not the stereotype of evil, etc. the merging of the two figures, their constant disintegration seems only partly successful, the great experiment of the gods—to add the command of self-love to that of 'love thy neighbour', to add to the 'do good unto others', the 'do good unto yourself'—had to be contrasted with the plot and yet at the same time govern it. the moral 'prestations' had to be socially motivated, yet they also had to be attributed to a particular ability (a particular talent, particular predisposition).

figures from the morality play. The water-seller Wang is the chorus/Everyman figure; the gods are like the angel sent to find one virtuous soul in the cities of Sodom and Gomorrah; Shu Fu the barber is the tempter/devil figure. The Chinese locale is used so that familiar actions and behaviour can be seen in unfamiliar surroundings. In the play Brecht is showing something akin to a modern pilgrim-prostitute's progress. Shen Te/ Shui Ta's movement from poverty to economic success is paralleled by the gods' gradual slide downwards. On their travels through the world they experience increasing hardships: their gift to Shen Te sets her on an upward path, but to maintain her position she has to resort to methods alien to her nature. By the end of the play she has grown increasingly aware of her isolation. 'Der böse Mensch' (the evil person) Shui Ta is rejected both by her friends and the gods (though as an exception they will permit his re-appearance once a month). 'Der gute Mensch' (the good person) Shen Te, whom the gods thought lost, but who, like the prodigal son, has returned from her 'journey into wrong-doing', is now surrounded by her friends again, yet alone in the face of the 'tödliche Gebote' (mortal commandments) of the gods.

Compared both with *Leben des Galilei* and *Mutter Courage*, *Der gute Mensch von Sezuan* makes more extensive use of some of the devices of the 'epic theatre'. The *Intermezzi* showing the exchanges between Wang and the gods break up the action, providing an opportunity for discussion and re-appraisal of incidents and actions already staged. Though some of Galileo's lengthy monologues are directed as much at the audience as at the characters in the play, he never steps outside his character. The songs in *Mutter Courage* represent a different level in the drama's action and do allow the actors to adopt a position slightly to one side of the characters they are portraying. But in *Der gute Mensch von Sezuan* Brecht uses a narrator, a flashback with commentary (Scene 8), sets two plots side by side, before bringing them together in a court scene (a technique he uses again in *Der kaukasische Kreidekreis*), and deliberately raises or lowers the level of the language by the alteration of straightforward, colloquial prose with song and irregular rhythmic verse. As, for instance, in Scene 4, where, after hearing of the injury Wang has suffered, Shen Te turns angrily on the bystanders, with reproaches directed both at them and the audience:

> Oh, ihr Unglücklichen!
> Euerm Bruder wird Gewalt angetan, und ihr kneift die
>   Augen zu!
> Der Getroffene schreit laut auf, und ihr schweigt?
> Der Gewalttätige geht herum und wählt sein Opfer
> Und ihr sagt: uns verschont er, denn wir zeigen kein
>   Missfallen.
> Was ist das für eine Stadt, was seid ihr für Menschen!
> Wenn in einer Stadt ein Unrecht geschieht, muss ein
>   Aufruhr sein
> Und wo kein Aufruhr ist, da ist es besser, dass die Stadt
>   untergeht
> Durch ein Feuer, bevor es Nacht wird![1] (*GW 4*, p. 1536)

In lines 2–4 Brecht makes use of one of the favourite devices of classical rhetoric, the *tricolon abundans*: his verse and declamatory prose often employ this technique, clearly a relic from his own fondness for the classics. Here he balances the description of the situation with a registration of the lack of emotion and interest displayed by the onlookers. Man's indifference to the fate and misery of his fellow man is a recurrent theme in his work, here given poignancy and directness by the contrast of Shen Te's feeling for Wang and for mankind at large with the others' refusal to concern themselves. And, following on the anguished cry ('Was ist das . . .') comes the extended sentence which first states what *should* be the reaction to injustice, and then, in a plunging series of qualifying clauses and phrases

---

[1] Oh you unhappy wretches!
Your brother is treated brutally and you screw your eyes shut!
The sufferer cries aloud and you are silent?
The man of blood roams about selecting his victims
And you say: He spares us, for we show not the face of displeasure.
What sort of town is that, what sort of people are you!
When in a town injustice is done, there must be a revolt,
And where there is no revolt, then it is better if the town is swallowed up
By a raging fire before night falls!

which break up the flow of the verse yet inexorably drag the listener with them, calls for the destruction of that city where insensibility and unconcern squat like sleeping dwarfs.

Where the language of *Leben des Galilei* reflects the opposition between the past and the present, the shrugging off of old ideas and the putting on of the new, the language and imagery in *Der gute Mensch* capture the crass contrast between 'das Gute' and 'das Böse'. In the play, these are not absolute values, nor do they represent two distinct, subjective, moral or ethical tendencies—what Brecht refers to as the 'zwei seelen' (twin souls) principle. 'The evil cousin' Shui Ta, in his relationship with others, applies those very rules of conduct and behaviour that 'the good' Shen Te had experienced during her life in the gutter. She had observed the law of the jungle, the 'homo homini lupus' code: but, as Shen Te, she refuses to follow this code, since, as Shu Fu says, 'it is the young lady's nature to do good.' Yet the experience gained as Shen Te is put to good use by Shui Ta. And in one of the most brutal presentations of the denial of the efficacy of *Nächstenliebe* (love of one's neighbour) Shui Ta singles out the emotion of *Liebe* (love) as being the most dangerous of all. Ironic indeed, since Shen Te normally deals in *körperliche Liebe* (physical love) as a commodity, and yet is threatened by destruction when she feels genuine love for Sun:

> Die Zeiten sind furchtbar, diese Stadt ist eine Hölle, aber wir krallen uns an der glatten Mauer hoch. Dann ereilt einen von uns das Unglück: er liebt. Das genügt, er ist verloren. . . .

> Die Liebkosungen gehen in Würgungen uber.
> Der Liebesseufzer verwandelt sich in den Angstschrei.
> Warum kreisen die Geier dort?
> Dort geht eine zum Stelldichein![1]   (*GW 4*, p. 1546)

---

[1] The times are terrible, this town is Hell, but we claw our way up the smooth wall. Then one of us is overtaken by misfortune itself: he is in love. That suffices, he is lost . . .

The caresses melt into strangleholds.
The sigh of love is transformed into a cry of fear.
Why are the vultures circling over there?
There someone is going to a rendezvous.

The four lines of verse emphasize the nature of the shifting barriers between love and cruelty: the surroundings cause gestures of love to become their opposite. Man's wish for goodness is thwarted by a society which depends on the exploitation of the individual.

None of the mature dramas presents a solution, though each signposts the path towards it. Each is, in its way, open-ended, though this aspect is more obvious in *Der gute Mensch von Sezuan*, where the epilogue states quite openly that the ending is unsatisfactory—for those, that is, who want to see all knots neatly tied together. Brecht's view of the function of the theatre, of the nature of his drama and the role of the audience is encompassed by four lines from this epilogue, which yet again emphasize the antithetical aspects of his style:

> Wir stehen selbst enttäuscht und sehn betroffen
> Den Vorhang zu und alle Fragen offen.
> (. . .)
> Verehrtes Publikum, los, such dir selbst den Schluss!
> Es muss ein guter da sein, muss, muss, muss![1]

> (*GW 4*, p. 1607)

The final line, though perhaps more memorable for the obviousness of the rhyme than the aptness of the conviction, is nevertheless an urgent and pressing declaration of Brecht's own wishes, and of the need to solve the dilemma which splits man and divides society.

[1] We ourselves stand disappointed and behold in consternation
The curtain closed and every question unresolved.
(. . .)
Dear members of the audience, off you go, find your own ending!
There must be a good one, must, must, must!

5

Comedy, Farce and Satire

Herr Puntila und sein Knecht Matti (Mr Puntila and His Man, Matti)

Having succeeded in giving *Der gute Mensch von Sezuan* a more or less final shape, Brecht, with his usual unflagging zeal for new projects, set about completing the comedy *Herr Puntila und sein Knecht Matti*. Adapting a play of Hella Wuolijoki's, Brecht sets out to show the relationship between the landowner Puntila and his servant-chauffeur Matti. Puntila can glow with bonhomie providing he already glows with alcohol, and in his various escapades—hiring workmen, making assignations with four women for the same day or sabotaging his daughter's engagement to a diplomat so that she can marry Matti—we find ourselves laughing with the capitalist who, sober, is less endearing. When the alcohol wears off he is blessed with total lack of recall, and can thus fire the workmen, spurn the four women and react with horror at the thought of a mere chauffeur marrying his daughter. Yet essentially Puntila's nature is not changed by drink: he is no less acquisitive, self-centred or domineering when drunk than when sober. Just more entertaining. Matti gradually tires of the situation and after one of the comic highpoints in Brecht's work—the climbing of the Hatelma-mountain (in reality a collection of tables, chairs and bottles)—decides to leave Puntila's service.

Writing on 14 September 1940, Brecht notes:

> der aufriss hat seine beschränkungen von der vorlage her, und der schweyk-ton setzt ebenfalls grenzen, aber das

ganze macht vergnügen und ist eine erholung nach dem
sezuan-stück.[1]   (*AJ*, p. 169)

The *schweyk-ton* is one of the essential ingredients in all Brecht's
dramas where comedy and comic dialogue play important parts
—it is a tone to be found in *Mutter Courage* as well as in
Der aufhaltsame Aufstieg des Arturo Ui (The Resistible Rise
of Arturo Ui) and *Schweyk im zweiten Weltkrieg* (Schweyk
in the Second World War). It is, in fact, the comic element
which links the two latter works with *Puntila*, while the character of the rich landowner who radiates charity and goodwill
when drunk, and displays callousness and indifference when
sober, is a modification of the dual personality theme of *Der
gute Mensch von Sezuan*. The comedy in *Puntila* is a great deal
warmer and more realistic than the grotesque and farcical
extravagances of *Arturo Ui*, though both works display the
influence of Chaplin on Brecht's work. The friendship between
Chaplin's drunken millionaire and the little tramp in *City
Lights* is reflected in the Puntila–Matti relationship. (There is
incidentally another, less obvious, parallel: Brecht's interest
in P. G. Wodehouse leads him to draw on the Bertie Wooster–
Jeeves relationship for various aspects of the master–servant
situation in the play.) And Chaplin's Adenoid Hynkel in
The Great Dictator clearly provided Brecht with a number of
useful ideas for his characterization of Ui—though, like others,
he had for some time been aware of the theatrical possibilities
of the resemblance of Hitler to Chaplin's tramp.

Der aufhaltsame Aufstieg des Arturo Ui (The Resistible Rise of Arturo Ui)

It has been customary to consider *Arturo Ui* second-rate
Brecht: it is high time to revise this opinion. In terms of sheer
dramatic impact, it loses little in comparison with the 'accepted'
masterpieces: and there are individual scenes where Brecht

[1] the draft has its limitations inherited from the original model and the
schweyk-tone likewise sets up barriers, but i find the whole thing enjoyable
and it's a relaxation after the sezuan-play.

achieves a quite unique combination of farce and horror. Like
Der gute Mensch, the drama is a parable, this time treating
Hitler's rise to power as a gangster show, and setting the events
of recent history in Al Capone's Chicago. The Hitler–Capone–
Ui analogies are central not only to Brecht's characterization
of Ui but also to the plot: incidents from Hitler's rise to power
are directly related to stages from Capone's career. The Night
of the Long Knives corresponds, in Brecht's play, to the St
Valentine's Day massacre; the Reichstag trial, together with
the falsified testimony, to trials involving Capone and suborned
witnesses; the annexation of Cicero (=Austria) to the actual
taking over of the area of Cicero near Chicago. And the various
characters correspond not only to their German equivalents
(Dogsborough = Hindenburg; Giri = Goering; Roma =
Roehm; Givola = Goebbels, etc.) but also to various members of the Capone gang and others involved in the Chicago
rackets.

It is easy to criticize the work for its lack of 'moral indigna-
tion', for its daring to set the character of Hitler on a stage
considerably smaller than the one on which he was accustomed
to appear. And it is arguable whether Brecht's attempt to treat
these times comes anywhere near the appalling reality: but
what other way is there? At least Brecht's work, as well as
reducing Hitler in stature, strikes a note of horror which is
considerably more convincing than most other attempts to
present this era in terms of those at the top. Brecht's intention
is to cut the mighty criminals of history down to size, to expose
them as ridiculous, petty, clumsy clowns. His defence of this
approach is typical of his persuasive manipulation of dialectics:

> Die grossen politischen Verbrecher müssen durchaus
> preisgegeben werden, und vorzüglich der Lächerlichkeit.
> Denn sie sind vor allem keine grossen politischen Ver-
> brecher, sondern die Verüber grosser politischer Ver-
> brechen, was etwas ganz anderes ist.
>
> Keine Angst vor der platten Wahrheit, wenn sie nur wahr
> ist! Sowenig das Misslingen seiner Unternehmungen Hitler
> zu einem Dummkopf stempelt, so wenig stempelt ihn

der Umfang dieser Unternehmungen zu einem grossen
Mann.[1]   (*GW 17*, p. 1177)

It is tempting to accept this as the final statement on the
play's *raison d'être*, yet the argument smacks rather of sophistry. Brecht, in both *Arturo Ui* and his essays and notes on the
Hitler phenomenon, for the most part insisted on viewing him
in strictly Marxist terms as the logical if extreme throw-up of
the powers of imperialism and capitalism. Hence these forces
must also be portrayed as playing a role in his rise (they are
noticeably absent from *Schweyk im zweiten Weltkrieg*).
Furthermore, Brecht protests in the notes to *Arturo Ui* that
Hitler was not a 'grosser Mann': yet, discussing with Lion
Feuchtwanger the latter's presentation (in an article) of
Hitler as 'ein nichts, ein bedeutungsloses sprachrohr der
reichswehr, einen schauspieler, der den führer spielt usw' (a
nothing, a meaningless mouthpiece of the army, an actor playing at being the führer, etc.). Brecht counters that he *was* 'eine
persönlichkeit' (a personality) (*AJ*, p. 311). This presentation
and characterization of Hitler as a 'personality' is obvious in his
dramas: yet he appears to wish to play this factor down in his
theoretical writings. 'Dialectics' here seems more like per-
plexing paradox.

Arturo Ui owes much of its theatrical impact to its gangster
milieu; like all things American, this had fascinated Brecht,
and he himself acknowledged that he drew on his recollections
of the gangster films of the thirties (with Cagney, Raft and
Robinson) for the work's atmosphere. This world of mobsters,
machine guns and melodramatic menace is essential for the
play's satire. Without it, Brecht might well have made his
points as forcibly: but a quasi-documentary style would not
have assisted the savagery of the satire. Matthew Hodgart's

---

[1] The great political criminals just have to be exposed, and particularly
to ridicule. For above all they are not great political criminals, but the
perpetrators of great political crimes, which is something quite different.

No need to be afraid of the plain truth, provided it is true! The failure
of his undertakings no more marks Hitler off as an idiot than the scope of
these undertakings mark him off as a great man.

comments on the nature of satire are especially appropriate to this case:

> ... even more important is the element of fantasy which seems to be present in all true satire. The satirist does not paint an objective picture of the evils he describes, since pure realism would be too oppressive. Instead he usually offers us a travesty of the situation which at once directs our attention to actuality and permits an escape from it.

Chaplin has said that he would never have made *The Great Dictator* had he known the real state of affairs in Germany: Brecht would never have made such a statement, though he would have sympathized with the sentiment. His obstinate and simplistic insistence on viewing Hitler as a bastard off-shoot of capitalism annoyed his friends and still annoys some critics. Yet, if, as he himself maintains: 'the proof of the pudding is in the eating', then *Arturo Ui* succeeds where Chaplin thought he failed. Brecht's Ui is a clumsy, small-time crook who 'makes it in the big-time'. He is given to childish petulance, violent rages and theatrical gestures, and prefers a steam-shovel to a rapier when dealing with his enemies—in short, he displays most of Hitler's qualities in travestied form. But in his very ridiculousness lies his menace; his behaviour is at once comic and horrifying—nowhere more so than in one of Brecht's greatest scenes, where Ui takes lessons in acting and deportment. It is a piece of staggering theatrical ingenuity, presenting the process of Ui's transformation so convincingly that, in the dramatist's distorting mirror, one sees Ui slipping into a role which for all its fantastic pantomimic elements, nevertheless overlaps with the historical identity.

Schweyk im zweiten Weltkrieg (Schweyk in the Second World War)

Where *Arturo Ui* achieves its effect by reducing the Nazis to gangster size and by presenting their crimes in terms of gang warfare and cauliflower trusts, *Schweyk im zweiten Weltkrieg* sets out to achieve a similar aim with different methods. Here, two levels run through the play: the 'höhere Regionen' (higher regions) where Hitler and his satraps discuss their plans in bleating operatic arias; and the *Wirtshaus 'Zum Kelch'* (the 'Flagon' inn) where Schweyk and his friends regularly gather. The first seven scenes—distinct from the *Intermezzi*—are set in Prague. The dog-dealer Schweyk is arrested and brought to Gestapo headquarters: but he is soon released both because of his 'stupidity' and because he appears likely to be useful to Bullinger, the S.S. officer. A confused sub-plot involving the plan to kidnap a Pomeranian for Bullinger misfires and when it seems that Schweyk's friend Baloun may join the German army because it promises regular meals for his insatiable appetite, Schweyk arrives with a packet of meat—in reality the prize Pomeranian. He is arrested again and this time shipped off to the Russian front where, in an epilogue, we see the 'historical confrontation' with Hitler.

Brecht's satire is once again directed at Hitler, with the juxtaposition of the 'high' world of the Nazis with the 'low' world of the friends of Schweyk. Hašek's novel is probably the best anti-military satire ever written, and Brecht borrows Hašek's character and his technique to satirize not the Austro-Hungarian military establishment but the Nazi system. Yet the mood of the work (as well as its form) marks it off as a comedy rather than an extended dramatic satire: the element of fantasy, so important in *Arturo Ui*, is less in evidence here, and Brecht's Prague is more realistic, the characters more earthy and recognizably human than his Chicago gangsters.

Schweyk embodies, in a more positive form, the little man's urge for survival that Brecht had already portrayed in *Mutter Courage*. But, in the course of the play, this comes to be seen as something more—namely, the means whereby the little man can oppose the power of Hitler. Whether such an interpretation is consistent with the character either of Hašek's or of Brecht's Schweyk is a question on which critics adopt radically different positions. It is one thing to present Schweyk as an 'accidentally-on-purpose' bungler or a deliberately simpleminded stooge, carrying out orders which achieve the opposite result of what was intended. In these cases, his instinct for survival and for making the best of a situation will see him through and at the same time allow the author plenty of opportunity for satirizing the system. But to see in Schweyk *the* embodiment of that force which can oppose Hitler is to attempt to impose Hašek's picture and interpretation of an historical situation on another where different laws prevail. It displays a strange lack of awareness of the historical dialectic, as well as inviting criticism for its over-simplification.

It is difficult to suppress several reservations about Brecht's view of the little man who unintentionally/intentionally throws several spanners in the works of Hitler's war machine. One obvious objection is that, unlike Hašek's representatives of the Austro-Hungarian military system, the Nazis would not have worn Schweyk's behaviour for longer than it took them to bundle him off to the nearest concentration camp. Speaking in 1938 of the problems of Realism, Brecht could write: 'Ein Rat "Schreibt wie Shelly!" wäre absurd' (A piece of advice 'Write like Shelley!' would be absurd) (*GW 19*, p. 349). Yet his own practice in *Schweyk im zweiten Weltkrieg* is not far removed from this. He borrows Hašek's Schweyk—his attitudes, his behaviour—and, discarding his surroundings, winds him up and pushes him into a world totally unlike that where he found him. This is, to be sure, not unusual in Brecht's work. But the essential difference is that here, the alterations to Schweyk's character are so minor that we are expected to accept that history has stood still and that Brecht's Schweyk can practise the same methods as his predecessor of three decades earlier. The militarism of the declining years of the Austro-Hungarian Empire, with its comparatively ordered structure, bears little resemblance to the world of the S.S. and the German *Wehrmacht* (Armed Forces). Hašek's Schweyk could function in the military world *of his time*: Brecht obviously had reservations about his ability to make the military world of the Nazis similarly acceptable, and hence he begins by 'demilitarizing' his Schweyk. To no avail: Schweyk *has* to function in military surroundings, so Brecht brings him in by the back door, while endeavouring to retain Hašek's approach. He should have heeded his own words:

Das kämpfende, die Wirklichkeit ändernde Volk vor

Augen, dürfen wir uns nicht an erprobte Regeln des
Erzählers, ehrwürdige Vorbilder der Literatur . . . klam-
mern.[1]   (ibid., p. 325)

A comedy like *Schweyk im zweiten Weltkrieg* which aims at
realism, should observe as one of the basic rules of the genre
the principle that the play itself lays down: 'Es wechseln die
Zeiten' (The times are changing). Or, to use Brecht's own words
once again:

Mit dem gleichen Spiegel kann man in der Literatur
nicht andere Epochen spiegeln . . .[2]   (ibid., p. 359)

Though there are these weaknesses in the play's argument,
the sheer theatricality of the work tends to push them into the
background. Schweyk's own irrepressible nature is reflected
in the play's overall mood: Brecht's sure sense of atmosphere
and character enables him to give dramatic form to that
Schweykian endurance and tenacity which effectively counter
both the feelings of despair to which the characters occasionally
succumb and the untiring machinations of the Brettschneiders
in the Nazi system. It is Schweyk's endurance, his stolid, dumb
immovability which Brecht wishes the audience to see as the
means of thwarting the Nazis' grandiose, non-stop planning
and their over-zealous efficiency. In such a context, any attempt
to view Brettschneider and his lackeys as muddle-headed fools
goes against both the text and Brecht's view of the contradictions in the historical situation. Schweyk is like a large rock
thrown into a narrow, swift-running stream: the stream's
course changes, in the same way as his practised inability to
co-operate in effect changes the Nazis' plans for 'the little
man'. It is not accidental that the theme of change receives its
most effective realization in Scene 6 where, after Frau Ko-
pecka has been brutally beaten by Bullinger, the S.S. officer,
she returns to her counter and sings 'Das Lied von der Moldau' (The Song of the Moldau). The song expresses the es-

---

[1] Keeping before our eyes the struggling people who change reality,
we must not cling to tried and tested rules for the narrator, and venerable
literary models.

[2] In literature, one cannot reflect different epochs with the same mirror.

sence of the play's (and its author's) belief in the inevitability
of change. It is one of the most powerful moments in all of
Brecht's dramas, at once moving and encouraging. The world
of the inn, which seems sheltered from the brutality of the
outside world, is invaded by this brutality, and the resolute
mood of cheerfulness shattered. But the song which closes the
scene re-establishes a sense not of cheap, safe hopes, but of an
enduring conviction:

> Das Grosse bleibt gross nicht und klein nicht das Kleine.
> Die Nacht hat zwölf Stunden, dann kommt schon der Tag.[1]
> *(GW 5*, p. 1968)

As well as referring *back* to the incident in the scene, the
song refers *forward* to the immediately following *Zwischen-
spiel* (intermezzo) where Hitler and von Bock make plans for
the invasion of the Soviet Union. The conviction that their
plans will succeed is balanced by the song's assertion that
might cannot endure. And the complete collapse of Hitler's
Reich, built for a thousand years, is foreshadowed in the
grotesque fantasy at the end of the play where, lost in a
howling snowstorm, Hitler and Schweyk come face to face.
'Der kleine Mann', in whom Hitler places his trust, shows
at the end of the play that the grand plans will come to
nothing. The grim, nightmarish atmosphere of this scene
where the two worlds of Hitler and Schweyk are finally
brought together, contrasts sharply with what has gone before.
Hitler, lost in the wastes of Russia, has already lost the war:
the thousand-year *Reich* is collapsing, and the 'überlebens-
grosse Figur' (figure larger than life) becomes a grotesquely
clumsy, unco-ordinated marionette. The superiority of
Schweyk's own common sense has thwarted the plans of the
Germans, and it is summed up in the crude contempt of his
final words to Hitler:

> Und ich sags dir ganz offen, dass ich nur noch nicht
> weiss

---

[1] The mighty do not always remain so, nor the small always small.
The night has twelve hours and then comes the day.

Ob ich auf dich jetzt schiess oder fort auf dich
scheiss.[1] (*GW 5*, p. 1993)

It is a slightly cheap joke, familiar to most English students of
German and could hardly be considered an adequate verifica-
tion of Shakespeare's

Not marble, nor the gilded monuments
Of princes, shall outlive this powerful rhyme!

[1] And I tell you quite frankly that I simply don't know
Whether to shoot at or shit on you.

6

The Later Plays

Der kaukasische Kreidekreis (The Caucasian Chalk Circle)

Like both *Arturo Ui* and *Schweyk*, *Der kaukasische Kreidekreis* was intended for an American audience. None achieved what Brecht had hoped for: the earlier two never reached the stage, while *Der kaukasische Kreidekreis* received its first performance in Minnesota! It was not the Broadway opening Brecht had banked on when he first suggested the play to Luise Rainer. Yet it remains—especially with English-speaking audiences—the most popular of the later plays. The reasons are not hard to find: the panoramic character of the work, the 'fairy-tale' elements (though these are far more doubled-edged than they appear at first glance), the characters of Grusche and Azdak and the familiar combination of the poetic and the commonplace. Brecht was well aware of the play's individual position in his *oeuvre*. In a diary note from 1949 he puts his finger on what it is that will attract future audiences:

> eigentliche repertoirestücke, d.h. stücke, die nahezu immer gegeben werden können, weil sie im thema sehr allgemein sind und den theatern gelegenheiten für ihre allgemeinsten künste gewähren, gibt es bei den deutschen wenige . . . von meinen stücken haben diesen charakter vermutlich nur die *Dreigroschenoper* und der *Kreidekreis*.[1]
>
> (*AJ*, p. 911)

Brecht was later to protest that 'Der kaukasische Kreidekreis

---

[1] the germans have very few actual repertory pieces i.e. plays that can be performed almost always, because their theme is very general and they provide the theatres with opportunities for their most general skills . . probably only the *Threepenny Opera* and *The Chalk Circle* of my plays have this characteristic.

ist keine Parabel' (The Caucasian Chalk Circle is not a parable)
(*GW 17*, p. 1205); and it is clearly not a parable of the same
order as *Arturo Ui* and *Der gute Mensch von Sezuan*. But its
structure and plot are certainly closer to the traditional parable
than to any other literary form, especially when it is recalled
that the judgement/mother-child motif has its roots in the
biblical story. If one defines a parable as a didactic tale that
presents a general moral truth or realization by means of an
analogy drawn from another sphere, it is a definition that is
readily applicable to *Der kaukasische Kreidekreis*—though in
this case it would be more appropriate to speak of a moral *and*
social truth. Furthermore, the traditional parable does not
furnish a model that corresponds in *every* detail with the
reality, but singles out *one* particular aspect for examination
and illustration. (It is the *fable* which is intended to correspond
in *every detail* with reality: in view of this, Brecht's own use of
the term 'parable'—when applied to *Arturo Ui*—appears to be
the result of some confusion in his own mind.) However, his
own (decidedly individual) view of the 'parable' genre becomes
clearer as his explanation continues:

> Genauer besehen aber enthüllt sich die Fabel als eine
> wirkliche Erzählung, die in sich selber nichts beweist,
> lediglich eine bestimmte Art von Weisheit zeigt, eine
> Haltung, die für den aktuellen Streitfall beispielhaft sein
> kann ... Das Theater darf also nicht die Technik benutzen,
> die es für die Stücke vom Parabeltypus ausgebildet hat.[1]
>
> (*GW 17*, p. 1205)

The insistence on viewing the play merely as an illustration of
a particular attitude seems perilously close to throwing the
baby out with the bath water, but it is the final sentence which
shows why Brecht is so concerned with problems of definition.
His argument leads to this point: it is not so much a question

---

[1] Looked at more closely however, the plot reveals itself to be a real tale,
which in itself proves nothing, but simply demonstrates a particular kind
of wisdom, an attitude which can be exemplary for the current dispute.
The theatre then cannot use the technique developed for plays of the
parable type.

of 'literary' distinctions and terminology but rather of the appropriateness of a particular theatrical style to a drama.

As in *Der gute Mensch von Sezuan* and *Schweyk im zweiten Weltkrieg*, Brecht builds the play round two plots. A prologue establishes a frame for the play proper: two Soviet collective farms are meeting to decide which shall receive ownership of a certain valley. The story of the chalk circle is then presented as an entertainment and an illustration of 'old wisdom'. After the fall of the paramount prince, all the governors of Grusinia are executed, including Georgi Abaschwili. His wife escapes, leaving behind their child, whom the new rulers are seeking. But Grusche, the maid, takes the child and after many dangers reaches relative safety in the mountains where she cares for the child as if it were her own. Here she is forced—for protection and respectability—to marry a dying peasant who recovers as soon as he hears that the war is over. When Simon, the soldier to whom she is engaged, returns from the wars and hears her claim the child as her own, he turns his back on her.

Parallel to this story and told in flashback runs the plot centred on the figure of Azdak, the former village scribe who has been appointed judge. When the earlier overthrow is reversed, the Governor's wife institutes a search for the child and the case is eventually heard by Azdak. A variation of the judgement of Solomon is used to decide the case: the child is placed in a chalk circle, Grusche refuses to take part in the tug-of-war for fear of hurting it, and Azdak sees in her the genuine maternal spirit. He gives her custody of the child and divorces her from her peasant husband so she can marry Simon, before vanishing forever.

Features normally associated with the parable are to be found both in Grusche, the story of her flight and the final judgement, and Azdak, the judge whom Brecht sees as a disillusioned revolutionary, and 'der niedrigste . . . aller richter' (the lowest of all judges). Speaking of Grusche, Brecht could claim in a rehearsal discussion that: 'Es handelt sich also weniger um eine "edle" Grusche als um eine praktisch veranlagte Frau' (It's less a question of a 'noble' Grusche than of a *practical* woman). But more accurate—and honest—is a note which describes the character in the following terms:

> die grusche sollte, indem sie den stempel der zurückge-
> bliebenheit ihrer klasse trägt, weniger identifikation
> ermöglichen und so als in gewissem sinn tragische figur
> (<das salz der erde>) objektiv dastehen.[1] (*AJ*, p. 662)

Any character intended to embody a particular human quality is clearly being assigned a parabolical role by the author.

Like *Der gute Mensch von Sezuan*, the play is concerned with posing a series of basic human questions seen within both a moral and a social context: legal justice versus practical justice; rightness versus expediency; good versus evil; new values versus established values; reason and feeling versus sentimentality; the claims of the natural mother versus those of the adoptive mother. Put thus, the arguments of the play might seem straightforward to the point of naïveté, particularly since the text is dotted with apt epigrams in which the relative claims of each side are summed up in lapidary language. But the audience is intended to examine each position critically: below the surface of a remark which convinces by virtue of its terse simplicity lies a complex of issues. Brecht provides us with a grid for these issues by advancing other arguments which relativize the initial remark, as in the *Vorspiel* (Prologue):

> *Der Alte rechts:* Nach dem Gesetz gehört uns das Tal.
> *Die junge Traktoristin:* Die Gesetze müssen in jedem Fall
> überprüft werden, ob sie noch stimmen.[2]

And:

> *Der Alte rechts:* Dieses Tal hat uns seit jeher gehört.
> *Der Soldat:* Was heisst 'seit jeher'? Niemandem gehört
> nichts seit jeher.[3] (*GW 5*, p. 2003)

---

[1] grusche ought to allow less identification in as much as she carries the stamp of the backwardness of her class and thus she ought to stand there objectively as a tragic figure in a sense (<the salt of the earth>).

[2] *The old man on the right:* According to the law the valley belongs to us. *The young tractor driver:* The laws must be examined in every case to see if they still hold.

[3] *The old man on the right:* This valley has belonged to us from the beginning of time.
The Soldier: What do you mean 'from the beginning of time'? Nobody owns anything from the beginning of time.

This dialectical pattern—already noted with reference to *Leben des Galilei*—runs through *Der kaukasische Kreidekreis*. The connection between the *Vorspiel* and the *Kreidekreis-Fabel* (Chalk-circle plot) is an illustration of the past–present relationship; while the *Hauptspiel* (play proper) itself opens with a description of poverty, exploitation and misery, and closes on a note of qualified optimism.

The 'Sänger' (Singer)

Once more Brecht's gift for encompassing an entire social setting within a few lines is exemplified in the antithetical and parallel lay-out of the *Sänger*'s opening address:

> In alter Zeit, in blutiger Zeit
> Herrschte in dieser Stadt, 'die Verdammte' genannt
> Ein Gouverneur mit Namen Georgi Abaschwili.
> Er war reich wie der Krösus.
> Er hatte eine schöne Frau.
> Er hatte ein gesundes Kind.
> Kein andrer Gouverneur in Grusinien hatte
> So viele Pferde an seiner Krippe
> Und so viele Bettler an seiner Schwelle
> So viele Soldaten in seinem Dienste
> Und so viele Bittsteller in seinem Hofe.
> Wie soll ich euch einen Georgi Abaschwili beschreiben?
> Er genoss sein Leben.[1] (ibid., p. 2008)

The word *geniessen* (to enjoy), which in the mouths of characters such as Baal or Galileo has more positive associations, here

[1] In ancient times, in bloody times
There reigned in this city, called 'The Damned',
A governor named Georgi Abaschwili.
He was rich as Croesus.
He had a beautiful wife.
He had a healthy child.
No other governor in Grusinia had
So many horses in his stable
And so many beggars on his threshold
So many soldiers in his service
And so many suppliants at his court.
How am I to describe to you a figure such as Georgi Abaschwili?
He enjoyed his life.

sums up the smug exploitation of the poor by the rich. Every remark in this opening speech is qualified in negative terms by its fellow. The historical setting is established, its laws of cruelty and blood, and no attempt is made to elaborate on the facts. The details are kept deliberately simple and basic, and the pomp and richness of the court are described in terms of possessions—*Pferde* (horses), *Soldaten* (soldiers), even the wife and children. Set against these are the people who suffer while the mighty prosper. It is one of Brecht's most effective introductions, not only because of its immediate relevance to the scene, but because it establishes a view of a situation which will run through the play.

In the play the *Sänger* fills several roles: he is stage-manager, commentator, chorus, a deliverer of monologues, and a controller of the course of the action in much the same way as the reader in the Bunraku puppet-plays. Sometimes these roles overlap, sometimes they follow one another within particular scenes. He is intended as an anti-illusionary device and is, in this sense, the most extreme embodiment since the *Lehrstücke* of an epic rather than a dramatic principle. At the same time he is also a three-dimensional character—not of course *involved* in the 'Kreidekreis' plot as are Grusche and Azdak— who is intended to stand as a reminder of the connection between the past of the *Hauptspiel* and the present of the *Vorspiel*. But is this really kept before the audience? Or—to put it another way, how essential is the *Vorspiel* to the play itself? As a point of reference, its *function* is clear. One cannot object to the arguments advanced in the *Vorspiel*: the debate between the two sides is neither dull nor clichéd, and the *Vorspiel* itself no mere pandering to Communist sensibilities.

Yet the characters bear an uncomfortable resemblance to the heroes and heroines of Socialist Realism, noble comrades in the cause of a better future. And, in spite of the differences of opinion, the general atmosphere is one of cosy chattiness: 'we're all good Socialist chums really, let's not get excited'. It's rather like enacting a proletarian equivalent of an urbane board meeting where bread and cheese instead of the port are being circulated. But Brecht would have been better to lift the tempo of the exchanges: the arguments and counter-arguments carry weight, but their advocates hardly press them home with any persistence. The young Stefan Brecht's objections that the conflict could be more real and tougher might well have received more consideration.

Grusche and Azdak

It is, however, the characters of Grusche and Azdak who provide the focal point for the play's theme, and in this respect, *Der kaukasische Kreidekreis* is something of a rarity in Brecht's works. In no other play has he created two such dominating protagonists, so similar in their vitality and conviction. Grusche, in assuming responsibility for the child, performs an isolated act which cannot have any great impact on society. But Azdak, the good/bad judge, is set in a position where his judgements can redress the balance in society—if only for a short time. Azdak embodies Brecht's fondness for paradox and contradiction in a more extreme form than Grusche. He could even be seen as representing Brecht's own reservations about the goodness of Grusche. For she is the only character in Brecht's dramas for whom goodness pays off—yet it requires the assistance of a most unlikely *deus* (or rather *advocatus*) *ex machina* to see to it that she wins the case. Goodness is not its own reward—not that Grusche asks for this: but it is only the 'verkommenste(r) aller richter' (the most depraved of all judges) who can prevent the disasters implied in the *Sänger*'s cry 'Schrecklich ist die Verführung zur Güte' (Terrible is the temptation to goodness) (ibid., p. 2025).

By the time we come to the final scene of the play, Azdak, whose self-interest has organized his own survival in such bloody and confused times, can afford an interest in the fate of others worse off than himself and incapable of defending themselves. Earlier he had acted according to his interpretation of the spirit of law, now he even goads Grusche to defend herself. But to see Azdak only as a Schweyk who merely twists the law to suit the situation is to view Brecht's characterization in unnecessarily simple terms. As one of the soldiers says when Azdak is appointed judge: 'Immer war der Richter ein Lump, so soll jetzt ein Lump der Richter sein' (The judge was always a scoundrel, so now a scoundrel shall be the judge) (ibid., p. 2078). Azdak is not a cunning beggar with a heart of gold, he is, in Brecht's words, self-seeking and parasitic, and therefore:

> so übt er weiter bürgerliches recht, nur verlumptes, sabotiertes, dem absoluten eigennutz des richtenden dienstbar gemachtes.[1] (*AJ*, p. 650)

Seen thus, he becomes a far more contradictory and hence more individual and complex figure—not simply a poor man's Solomon. Grusche embodies practical goodness, Azdak a practical *modus vivendi* based on both self-interest and a concern for manipulating the system to accommodate the wishes of others. Goodness needs to be balanced by shrewdness, a degree of cynicism and determination.

And in the outcome of the trial of the chalk circle lies the lesson not only for the inhabitants of the Kolchos but for the audience as well. The play closes on a note of optimism, though *not* with an implied assertion of the advent of Utopia:

> Und nach diesem Abend verschwand der Azdak und
>   ward nicht mehr gesehen.
> Aber das Volk Grusiniens vergass ihn nicht und gedachte
>   noch
> Lange seiner Richterzeit als einer kurzen
> Goldenen Zeit beinah der Gerechtigkeit.[2]
>
> (*GW 5*, p. 2105)

The biblical style of these lines—'he vanished and was seen no more'—coupled with the key word *beinah* (almost) underlines yet again the *märchenhaft* (legendary) qualities of the play, qualities which are uncomfortably balanced by the explicit

---

[1] thus he goes on administering middle-class justice, only it's a rascally sort of justice, sabotaged, made subject to the absolute self-interest of the person administering it.

[2] And after this evening Azdak disappeared and was seen no more. But the people of Grusinia did not forget him and Long remembered his time as judge as a short Golden age almost of justice.

moral of the last six lines. The idea that 'da gehören soll, was da ist, denen, die für es gut sind' (What is there should belong to those who are good for it) is praiseworthy, but closer to naïve wishful thinking than to the argumentative temper of drama.

Die Tage der Commune (The Days of the Commune); Turandot; Coriolan

Der kaukasische Kreidekreis is the last of those plays to display convincing evidence of Brecht's poetic and dramatic genius. *Die Tage der Commune* is not the success he hoped for. It is partly effective in its attempt to portray the problems of the Paris Commune. But its strangely conservative, even at times naturalistic style, and its praiseworthy but clumsy attempts to make *das Volk* (the people) the hero of the piece, mark it off as a decidedly lame piece of didactic drama—especially when compared with *Die Mutter* or the earlier *Lehrstücke*. It is colourful and never dull, but it resembles nothing so much as a rather poor Courbet canvas suddenly brought to life. Indicative perhaps of Brecht's own lack of conviction in the handling of his material is the fact that it is the scenes with the upper classes and the bourgeoisie which are by far the most effective. Yet once again—as in the final scene, where the bourgeoisie observe the carnage and destruction through their lorgnettes as if they were attending a fox-hunt—he shows that the simple tendentiousness of most of the play is partly compensated for by his undiminished theatrical inventiveness.

The same holds for his last completed work *Turandot oder der Kongress der Weisswäscher* (Turandot or the Congress of the Whitewashers). Given a stage and some extensive rewriting, he could have made it a lively and forceful satire, much in the vein of *Arturo Ui*, using its chinoiserie elements to great comic effect. The character of Gogher Gogh is essentially a Chinese offshoot of the Chicago gangster Arturo Ui. And it is at this point that the argument of the play starts to creak. Brecht's aim is to satirize and pour scorn on the intellectual whitewashers: those word-peddlers, represented at their best

(or rather worst) in the circuitous meanderings and convoluted
sophistry of the Adornos and Horkheimers of this world.
They were the original targets of Brecht's attack. But, although
the play's plot is based on the fall of the Weimar Republic, the
anti-intellectual satire can be seen to have wider application.
Namely, to all those intellectuals who think that their lofty
thoughts determine the progress of mankind. In their catch-
word 'Wissen ist Macht' (knowledge is power) Brecht ironically
twists Bacon's famous epigram. For the Tuis 'know' anything
and everything; theirs is a knowledge without any practical
or social application. They drop catchphrases as hens lay eggs,
sell their wares with even less style than do prostitutes, weave
tapestries of apophthegms whose garish colours blind the eye
to the flimsiness of the material.

In an age where Socialist and Capitalist bureaucracies depend
on the custom-built spokesman, Brecht's 'Tea House of the
august Tuis' has immediate relevance. The inconsequentialities
and false parallels of the theme, so crudely obvious in the latter
half of the play, are still offset by the ingenuities of the first
half. Nowhere more so than in Scene 4, where a pupil in the
Tuischule (Tui school) is instructed in the 'subtleties' of Tui-
reasoning in a wildly funny variation on the Tantalus motif.
Here it is a question of a *Brotkorb* (bread basket) which is
lowered or raised according to what might be called the
'credibility gap quotient' of the candidate's answers to certain
questions. As Kai-Ho's (Mao Tse Tung) arguments are more
and more distorted, the *Brotkorb* hovers ever lower over the
candidate's head. It is a comically grotesque inversion of that
relationship between *Fressen* (food) and *Moral* (morals/
ethics) which had first been stated in *Die Dreigroschenoper*:
'Erst kommt das Fressen, dann kommt die Moral' (Grub
first, then ethics) (*GW 2*, p. 457). Here it is rather: 'Komm
doch mit der gewünschten Moral, dann kriegst du zu fressen'
(Come up with the desired bit of ethics, then you'll get your
grub).

Brief mention must be made of the play Brecht seems to have
considered the most important of his later adaptations. His version of *Coriolanus* is intended in some measure as a re-ap-

praisal of Shakespeare's view of the hero. The role of the out-standing individual in an historical or fictional situation is a familiar theme in Brecht's work. And although his re-working of Shakespeare's play aims to show the people in a more positive and Coriolanus in a more negative light, he, nevertheless, does not butcher Shakespeare's text to suit his purposes. The notion of the dispensability of the hero and hence the increased im-portance of the role of the plebeians are already in Shakes-peare's play. Brecht began by over-emphasizing both aspects, but ended by accommodating the claims of both in much the same terms as he had already stated in 1951–2.

> Was das Vergnügen am Helden und das Tragische betrifft, müssen wir die blosse Einfühlung in den Helden 'Marcius' hinter uns bringen, um zu einem reicheren Vergnügen zu gelangen; wir müssen zumindest imstand sein, ausser der Tragödie des Coriolan auch die Tragödie Roms, ins-besondere des Plebs zu erleben.[1] (*GW* 17, p. 1252)

Later he was even to observe that the earlier alterations were perhaps not really necessary, given a skilful production. Had he, meanwhile, come to see the applicability to his own case of his oft-quoted 'Ich denke, wir können den Shakespeare ändern, wenn wir ihn ändern können' (I think we can alter Shakespeare if we *are able* to alter him)? (*GW 16*, p. 879). Perhaps he had finally become more convinced of the truth of another of his own remarks, made in discussion with reference to this play. It is always dangerous to assign to an isolated remark the status of a final statement on an author's outlook. Yet this one seems appropriate, not only for its reference to Coriolanus, but because it emphasizes once again where the origins of Brecht's theatrical style are to be found:

> Wir möchten den Spass haben und vermitteln, ein Stück durchleuchteter Geschichte zu behandeln. Und Dialektik zu erleben . . . Selbst in den Panoramen der Jahrmarkts-

---

[1] As far as the enjoyment of the hero and the nature of the tragic qualities are concerned, we must put behind us mere identification with the hero 'Marcius', in order to arrive at a deeper enjoyment: we must at least be in a position to experience also—apart from the tragedy of Coriolanus—the tragedy of Rome, in particular of the plebs.

schaubuden und in den Volksballaden lieben die einfachen Leute, die so wenig einfach sind, die Geschichten vom Aufstieg und Sturz der Grossen, vom ewigen Wechsel, von der List der Unterdrückten, von den Möglichkeiten der Menschen. Und sie suchen die Wahrheit, das 'was dahinter ist'.[1] (ibid., p. 888)

[1] We'd like to feel and communicate the sense of fun involved in treating a piece of history. And in experiencing dialectics in action . . . Even in the panoramas of the stalls at the fairs and in the popular ballads simple people—who are not in the least simple—love tales of the rise and fall of great men, of eternal change, of the cunning of the oppressed, of the possibilities of human beings. And they look for the truth—what is behind it all.

7

The Theory

Brecht's theoretical writings, related to or divorced from his plays, have been the subject of more disagreement than the dramas themselves. Essays and books on isolated questions such as the *V-Effekt* (Alienation Effect), *Gestus* (Gest), and 'epic theatre', or on the awe-inspiring theme of Brecht's aesthetic of the theatre continue to appear at a rate alarming to anyone who considers the works themselves more worthy of intensive scrutiny. The sight of Brecht critics scattering quantities of ink or verbiage in lieu of blood, and carrying off either a Pyrrhic victory or the promise of a later joust to determine the ultimate victor, has now become a familiar annual spectacle. It is an exercise remarkable both for its persistent perversity and for its tendentiousness. As long ago as 1959 John Willett made a plea for reason:

> Of course the theory remains worth studying, and it is full of suggestive ideas for anyone who understands Brecht's work. But all that is essential in it is apparent from Brecht's own practice in the theatre. The point can be grasped without the theory. It cannot be grasped from the theory alone. (p. 186)

It remains one of the sanest guidelines for any study of Brecht's theories: yet it is a cry which still goes largely unheard.

Contradictions and the 'Dialectic'

Though Brecht in the *Anmerkungen zur Oper Aufstieg und Fall der Stadt Mahagonny* (Notes on 'The Rise and Fall of the City of Mahagonny') drew up a scheme displaying what he saw as the crucial differences between the dramatic (=Aristotelian) and epic theatre, he immediately qualified his own opposing categories by declaring: 'Dieses Schema zeigt nicht absolute Gegensätze, sondern lediglich Akzentverschiebungen' (This table does not show absolute opposites, but only shifts in emphasis) (*GW 17*, p. 1009). In short, although by instinct a speculative thinker, he wished—at least at this stage (1930)— also to be a systematic philosopher of the theatre. In this dichotomy lie many of the problems and unanswered questions raised by Brecht's theories of the theatre. In this connection some ironic lines from an early poem and an early diary note are especially appropriate:

Ich habe immer so viel mit Grundsätzen auszustehen gehabt
Alles hat bei mir mit Grundsätzen angefangen
Der Tabak sowohl wie die Schnapsgewässer
Ich wollte zuerst reinen Mund halten und habe mich nur verschnappt . . .[1]　　　　　　　　　　(*GW 8*, p. 108)

Ein Mann mit einer Theorie ist verloren. Er muss mehrere haben, vier, viele! Er muss sie sich in die Taschen stopfen wie Zeitungen, immer die neuesten, es lebt sich gut zwischen ihnen, man haust angenehm zwischen den Theorien. Man muss wissen, dass es viele Theorien gibt, hochzukommen, auch der Baum hat mehrere, aber er befolgt nur eine von ihnen, eine Zeitlang.[2]
　　　　　　　　　　　　　　　　　　(*GW 18*, p. 10)

This fascination for contradiction and opposing theories remained with Brecht throughout his life: with his interest in

---

[1] Matters of principle have always given me a lot to worry about
For me everything started with principles, I'd say
Tobacco, for instance, as well as my taste for liquor
I really did want to keep quiet at first, but I gave myself away.

[2] A man with one theory is lost. He must have several, four, many! He must stuff them in his pockets like newspapers, always the newest ones, one can live well amongst them, one has a pleasant place to live amongst theories. One must know that there are many theories about getting to the top, even the tree has several, but it follows only one of them, for a particular period of time.

Marxism he could comfortably accommodate all under the sacred canopy of 'the dialectic'. It is a term which, by nature of the process it describes, is incapable of definition in the terms of formal logic. Walter Theimer, in his handbook *Der Marxismus* makes a call for caution in using the term:

> Ganz verstanden hat die Hegelsche Dialektik noch niemand, wahrscheinlich auch ihr Begründer nicht. Im Marxismus nimmt sie die Stellung des mystischen Zentralbegriffs ein, der in den meisten Relgionssystemen zu finden und stets mit der Aufhebung der Sätze von der Identität und vom Widerspruch verbunden ist. Jede Debatte mit einem Kommunisten endet damit, dass der zweifelnde Gesprächspartner die Mitteilung erhält, er denke eben nicht dialektisch.[1]   (p. 31)

One is strongly reminded of Max Frisch's own comments on Brecht's methods of dialectical argumentation:

> Meinerseits habe ich dort, wo Brecht mit seiner Dialektik mattsetzt, am wenigsten von unserem Gespräch; man ist geschlagen, aber nicht überzeugt.[2]   (*T. 1.*, p. 210)

Many of Brecht's own contradictory pronouncements on the theatre are frequently the result not of a Marxist 'dialectical' method but of a simple addiction to paradox and to traditional dialectics, which were concerned with the investigation of various opinions from every possible standpoint. (A harsher view might also be that there is frequently evidence of some rather muddled thinking!) His own illustrations of 'dialectics' or of the 'dialectical method' show that for him dialectics is a constantly moving, constantly changing *process*, an awareness of contradictions: it is '(die) Lehre vom Fluss der Dinge' (the teaching of the flux of things) (*GW 18*, p. 237). When

---

[1] No one has yet completely understood Hegelian dialectics, probably not even its originator. In Marxism it occupies the position of the mystical central concept, which is to be found in most systems of religion and which is always bound up with the 'preservation' of the articles of identity and contradiction. Every debate with a Communist ends with the doubting partner in the conversation being told he just cannot think dialectically.

[2] For my part, I get the least out of our conversation when Brecht checkmates you with his dialectics; you're beaten, but not convinced.

speaking of poems, he can criticize them for a lack of dialectical elements:

> Flach, leer, platt werden Gedichte, wenn sie ihrem Stoff seine Widersprüche nehmen, wenn die Dinge, von denen sie handeln, nicht in ihren lebendigen, das heisst allseitigen, nicht zu Ende gekommenen und nicht zu Ende zu formulierenden Formen auftreten.[1]   (*GW 19*, p. 394)

Instances of Brecht's practical application of the method to his own theatre and his own thinking can best be studied in the *Messingkauf* dialogues, the *Kleines Organon* and the long discussion of the opening scene of *Coriolan*, entitled *Die Dialektik auf dem Theater*.

In the *Messingkauf* dialogues, the actor takes the philosopher to task for his apparent insistence on the dispelling of emotion from the theatre. He sees him as making the following demands:

> Weg mit der Ahnung, her mit dem Wissen!
> Weg mit dem Verdacht, her mit der Überführung!
> Weg mit dem Gefühl, her mit dem Argument!
> Weg mit dem Traum, her mit dem Plan!
> Weg mit der Sehnsucht, her mit dem Entschluss![2]

To which the *Philosoph* replies:

> Ich habe mich kaum so entschieden ausgesprochen, was die Aufgabe der Kunst im allgemeinen betrifft. Ich habe mich gegen die umgekehrten Losungen gewendet: Weg mit dem Wissen, her mit der Ahnung und so weiter ... Warum sollte ich die Sphäre des Geahnten, Geträumten, Gefühlten stillegen wollen? Die gesellschaftlichen Probleme werden von den Menschen auch so

[1] Poems become flat, empty, trite, when they remove the contradictions from their material, when the things they deal with do not appear in their living forms—that is, forms that are many-sided, not rounded off and not capable of a finished formulation.

[2] Get rid of presentiment, bring in knowledge!
Get rid of suspecting, bring in conviction!
Get rid of feeling, bring in argumentation!
Get rid of dreaming, bring in planning!
Get rid of yearning, bring in determination!

behandelt. Ahnung und Wissen sind keine Gegensätze.
Aus Ahnung wird Wissen, aus Wissen Ahnung. Aus
Träumen werden Pläne, die Pläne gehen in Träume über.
Ich sehne mich und mache mich auf den Weg, und ge-
hend sehne ich mich.[1]   (*GW 16*, pp. 640–1)

Such attitudes surely give the lie to those critics who insist that
Brecht's theatre was concerned with the primacy of *Ratio*
(reason) over *Gefühl* (emotion). It is in the tension between
Ahnen (suspecting) and *Wissen* (knowing) that he sees the very
essence of art. This same insistence on shifting boundaries and
a fondness for contradiction is displayed in the *Kleines Organon*:

> Diese Methode behandelt, um auf die Beweglichkeit der
> Gesellschaft zu kommen, die gesellschaftlichen Zustände
> als Prozesse und verfolgt diese in ihrer Widersprüchlichkeit.
> Ihr existiert alles nur, indem es sich wandelt, also in
> Uneinigkeit mit sich selbst ist. Dies gilt auch für die
> Gefühle, Meinungen und Haltungen der Menschen, in
> denen die jeweilige Art ihres gesellschaftlichen Zusammen-
> lebens sich ausdrückt.[2]   (*GW 16*, p. 682)

Frequently Brecht's descriptions of elements in a work (and the
attitude of the public towards a character) as 'dialectical' display the same vocabulary and outlook as his definition of
terms such as 'realistisch' and the 'kritische Haltung' (critical
attitude) he asks of his public. Realistic writing is seen as 'das
Moment der Entwicklung betonend' (emphasizing the element

---

[1] I hardly made such a definite pronouncement on the nature of art's
task in general. I set myself against the reverse forms of those catchphrases:
get rid of knowledge, bring in presentiment, etc. . . . . Why should I want to
shut out the realm of what can be sensed, dreamed of and felt? Social
problems are tackled by people in these ways as well. Sensing and knowing
aren't opposites. Sensing can lead to knowing, and vice versa. Dreams can
give rise to plans, plans can merge into dreams. I yearn for something and
set out and still yearn while I'm on my way.

[2] In order to get at the mobility of society this method treats social
conditions as processes and pursues these in their contradictoriness.
Everything exists for it only in so far as it is changing, that is, in dis-
harmony with itself. This also holds for the feelings, opinions and attitudes
of human beings, in which the specific manner of their social intercourse
is expressed.

of development) (*GW 19*, p. 326); the realist as dealing not
only in sensuous impressions but

> . . . er begreift die Wirklichkeit, in ständigem Kampf gegen
> die Schematik, die Ideologie, das Vorurteil, in ihrer Viel-
> fältigkeit, Abgestuftheit, Bewegung, Widersprüchlichkeit.[1]
>
> (ibid., p. 372)

The Development of the Theory

Such ideas are a far cry from the extreme position Brecht had
assumed in the twenties and early thirties. But he had always
been concerned with a re-appraisal and re-functioning of the
comfortably bourgeois German theatre. He began with his
sharply outspoken attacks on the productions of Expressionist
and Classical dramas in Augsburg (for one of which he was
even sued by the offended female lead). But these early criticisms were determined by their journalistic form: effective,
accurate in their criticism, full of vigour and sharp wit, but not
so concerned with an analysis of the nature and function of a
new type of theatre. This came in the twenties, and was given
impetus both by the 'epic' production techniques of Erwin
Piscator, and by Döblin's theories on the distinction between
the 'dramatic' and 'epic' form of fiction. Of course, as Brecht
himself acknowledges, moves had already been made in this
direction by Shakespeare in his history plays, by French novel-
ists (Zola in particular), and even by the Naturalists. Brecht
derived his initially convoluted theories of the epic drama from
productions of his own works (e.g. *Mann ist Mann*, *Leben
Eduards des Zweiten*) and from the experiments of Piscator.
The characteristics of this type of production were: coolness,
clarity, an awareness of the uncertainty occasioned by contradictions, a chipping away of the monumental plaster that had
engulfed plays and productions, a sense of objectivity, and
above all a refusal to subsume the whole into the Wagnerian
concept of the *Gesamtkunstwerk* (total work of art). Brecht's

---

[1] He comprehends reality, in constant struggle against systematization
ideology, pre-judging; in all its diversity, gradation, movement, contradictoriness.

attempts to fit these elements into a theory led to an insistence
on coherent systematization which the theory itself fails to display. He was not alone in his experimental re-appraisal of the
nature and function of the work of art. His concern for essentials, for the basic patterns of human behaviour, the epic stance
and the presentation of man in all his contradictions has its
analogy in Döblin's comments in *Der Bau des Romans* (The
Structure of the Novel) (1929):

> Was nun irgendeinen erfundenen Vorgang, . . . in die
> (Sphäre) des spezifisch epischen Berichts hebt, das ist
> *das Exemplarische des Vorgangs und der Figuren* . . . Es
> sind da starke Grundsituationen, Elementarsituationen
> des menschlichen Daseins, die herausgearbeitet werden, es
> sind Elementarhaltungen des Menschen . . .   (p. 106)

> Bei allen epischen Werken grösseren Umfangs muss man
> wissen, es wird kein rundes, abgeschlossenes, vollkommen
> umgangenes Kunstwerk vorgesetzt . . .[1]   (p. 123)

It is but a brief step from here to Brecht's statement in the
Anmerkungen zu Mahagonny that the epic work proceeds 'in
Sprünge' (in leaps), and displays 'Trennung der Elemente'
(separation of the elements). Yet this essay and its interesting
arguments, so frequently cited as the *ultima ratio*, are but the
first step towards a theory which will soon modify the essay's
over-simplifications and its somewhat contrived 'opposing
categories'.

The events of the thirties, Brecht's lack of a stage, and the
development of his own dramatic style all contribute to the
modification of his theory—though in a shape which does not
comfortably accommodate the sometimes conflicting demands
of all three factors. But the most stimulating and entertaining
exposé of his theory comes in the *Messingkauf* dialogues.

---

[1] What it is that lifts any invented incident to the realm of the specific-
ally epic account is the exemplary quality of the incident and of the
figures . . . There the emphasis is on the working out of powerful basic
situations, elementary situations of human existence, elementary human
attitudes . . . With all epic works of a fairly large scope one needs to
realize that one is not being presented with a rounded, finished, fully
encompassed work of art.

Their formal structure—prompted by his reading of Galileo's *Discorsi*—makes for a theory that is not developed in terms of formal logic: yet the pattern of dialogue, monologues, digressions, illustrations and short scenes, makes for a picture of Brecht's view of the theatre which is at once more rewarding and wider-ranging than anything he had previously attempted. And, although the poems are not included in the *GW* edition as part of the theory, it would be wrong to consider them as merely incidental to the arguments of the dialogues. More concise and persuasive than the dialogues (which occasionally tend towards diffuseness and a wish to make half a dozen points before one has been fully grasped), they are remarkable illustrations of Brecht's skill at combining literary modes. Using poetic conventions and the poetic idiom, he examines the nature of, and presents situations common to, the drama. Nowhere in his theoretical works does Brecht better display the effective combination of instruction with entertainment. These poems, precisely because they compress the argument and work with concrete yet vivid images, allow the reader to experience the distinctive nature of Brecht's theatre as well as the violence of his objections to the theatre as a temple where false emotions, like incense, are used to stupefy the audience. Here he is on the 'Theater der Gemütsbewegungen' (Theatre of emotions):

> Unter uns, es erscheint mir ein verächtliches Gewerbe
> Durch Theaterspielen lediglich
> Die trägen Gemüter zu bewegen. Wie Masseure
> Kommt ihr mir vor, die in die allzu fetten
> Weichen wie in Teig greifen, so den Faulen
> Den Schmer abknetend.[1]   (*GW 9*, p. 774)

Or 'Über die Nachahmung' (On Imitation), a variation on the frequently paraded remark 'Zeigen ist mehr als Sein'

---

[1] Between ourselves, it seems to me a contemptible profession
To use the theatre solely in order to
Set limp feelings in motion. Masseurs
Are what you seem to me, sinking your fingers in the greasy
Flanks of your audience as in a lump of dough,
Kneading away at their heavy laziness.

(showing is more than being), which according to Brecht involves the actor's retaining something of his own attitudes to his work:

> Der nur Nachahmende, der nichts zu sagen hat
> Zu dem, was er nachahmt, gleicht
> Einem armen Schimpansen, der das Rauchen seines
>   Bändigers nachahmt
> Und dabei nicht raucht. Niemals nämlich
> Wird die gedankenlose Nachahmung
> Eine wirkliche Nachahmung sein.[1]   (ibid, p. 771)

Or finally, in 'Suche nach dem Neuen und Alten' ('In search of the new and old') where once again he insists on an awareness of opposing factors in both a play and a character, and where his indication of sympathy for Courage is set in its correct perspective:

> Die Hoffnungen der Händlerin Courage
> Sind den Kindern tödlich; aber die Verzweiflung
> Der Stummen über den Krieg
> Gehört zum Neuen. Ihre hilflosen Bewegungen
> Wenn sie die rettende Trommel aufs Dach schleppt
> Die grosse Helferin, sollen euch
> Mit Stolz erfüllen; die Tüchtigkeit
> Der Händlerin, die nichts lernt, mit Mitleid.[2]
>
>   (ibid., p. 794)

He who only imitates and has nothing to say
On what he imitates is like
A poor chimpanzee, who imitates his trainer's smoking
And does not smoke while doing so. For never
Will a thoughtless imitation
Be a real imitation.
[2] The hopes of Courage the trader
Are fatal for her children; but the desperation
Of the dumb girl about the war
Is part of something new. Her helpless movements
As she drags the rescuing drum on to the roof,
The great helper, should
Fill you with pride; the stamina
Of the trader who learns nothing, with pity.

Verfremdung

In Brecht's case the popular game of 'hunt the symbol' has re-appeared under a modified but no less dangerous guise as 'hunt the *V-Effekt*, or *Gestus*, or "epic" elements'. It is a classic instance of refusing to see the wood for the trees, of considering the part to be more important than the whole. These terms are not entries in a catechism of the theatre, nor precepts set in the tables of theatrical law. In both his work and his theory, Brecht was concerned with the problem of analysing the effect and function of the theatrical experience. But during the years which saw the writing of his greatest dramas as well as the most developed examination of his theory, he found himself, because of the lack of a stage, in no position to explore and modify the application of the apparently authoritative theoretical observations. A note from 1940—that is, the period when he was working both on the *Messingkauf* dialogues and his mature dramas —shows how acutely he felt this need:

> es ist unmöglich, ohne die bühne ein stück fertigzumachen, the proof of the pudding . . . wie soll ich feststellen, ob etwa die 6 szene des *Guten Menschen* noch die erkenntnis der li gung von dem (sozialen) grund der schlechtigkeit ihres freundes aushält oder nicht? nur die bühne ent-scheidet über die möglichen varianten.[1]   (*AJ*, p. 122)

Frequently, the theories read like recipes for a type of drama which he was moving towards, but never reached—which is not at all the same as stating that the theoretician and the dramatist were two separate and warring personalities. If he could not examine the validity of his theories in contact with a stage, what better way to examine them than within the quasi-theatrical framework of the *Messingkauf* dialogues? What most worried him about the Aristotelian system was the absence of a critical attitude in the audience. The demand for 'pitiable

[1] it is impossible to finish a play without a stage, the proof of the pudding . . . how am i to determine whether, for example, the 6th scene of *The Good Person* can still sustain li gung's awareness of the (social) reason for the baseness of her lover or not? only the stage can decide about the possible variants.

and fearful incidents' left no place for criticism of the nature
or reality of these incidents—though Brecht clearly felt uncomfortable when it came to explaining *why* this was not
so:

> es bereitet grosse theoretische schwierigkeiten, zu er-
> kennen, dass die nachbildungen der aristotelischen
> dramatik (der auf katharsiswirkung ausgehenden drama-
> tik) in ihrer praktibilität begrenzt sind durch ihre funktion
> (gewisse emotionen zu organisieren) und durch die dazu
> nötige technik (der suggestion) und dass der zuschauer
> damit in eine haltung gebracht wird (die der einfühlung),
> in der er eine kritische stellungnahme zu dem abgebildeten
> nicht gut einnehmen kann, d.h. desto weniger einnehmen
> kann, je besser die kunst funktioniert.[1]
>
> (*AJ*, pp. 189–90)

It is a commendable attempt to state his aims: but this rather
awkward summary hints at his difficulties in presenting in the
Messingkauf proper a more convincingly formulated argument.

His answer to the *Suggestionstechnik* (technique of suggestion), which allowed the audience to float off in a trance in-
duced by the play and its actors, was the *Verfremdungseffekt*.
A critical examination of the meaning and Brecht's application
of this term could occupy an entire book. In these circumstances it is wiser to let a selection of Brecht's remarks on the
term speak for themselves—though the possibility of confusion
is in no way diminished:

> Er (d.h. der V-Effekt) besteht darin, dass die Vorgänge
> des wirklichen Lebens auf der Bühne so abgebildet werden,
> dass gerade ihre Kausalität besonders in Erscheinung
> tritt und den Zuschauer beschäftigt. Emotionen kommen

---

[1] serious theoretical difficulties are involved in recognizing that the
representations of aristotelian dramatic art (that which leads to the effect
of catharsis) are limited in their practicability by their function (that of
organizing certain emotions) and by the technique necessary for this (that
of suggestion); and that the audience is thereby led to adopt an attitude
(that of empathy) in which they cannot effectively assume a critical stance
vis-à-vis what is represented, i.e. the better the art form functions, the less
chance they have of assuming such a stance.

auch durch diese Kunst zustande, und zwar ist es die Meisterung der Wirklichkeit, welche, durch diese Vorführungen ermöglicht, den Zuschauer in Emotionen versetzt. Der V-Effekt ist ein altes Kunstmittel, bekannt aus der Komödie, gewissen Zweigen der Volkskunst und der Praxis des asiatischen Theaters.[1]   (*GW 16*, p. 652)

Man muss hierin nichts besonders Tiefes, Geheimnisvolles suchen. Der Schauspieler braucht dabei nichts anderes zu tun, als von anderen Leuten getan wird, wenn sie etwas beschreiben, mit der Absicht, es beherrschbar zu machen. Es ist lediglich eine Methode, das Interesse auf das zu Beschreibende zu konzentrieren, es interessant zu machen . . . Gewisse Selbstverständlichkeiten werden so nicht selbstverständlich, freilich nur, um nun wirklich verständlich zu werden.[2]   (*GW 15*, p. 362)

What is clear from this latter passage is that the *V-Effekt* is intended to make the familiar appear strange, the strange appear familiar. As John Willett observed—and Brecht knew—it is not *all* that revolutionary an aim: it is 'exactly what Shelley meant when he wrote that poetry "makes familiar objects to be as if they were not familiar" ' (p. 177). And Johnson's words that in Pope's work 'new things are made familiar and familiar things are made new' are in the same vein; as, of course, is Hegel's famous observation: 'Das Bekannte is darum, weil es überhaupt bekannt ist, nicht erkannt' (The known, precisely because it is known, is not recognized). And one final remark should help dispel suggestions that the *V-*

[1] It (i.e. the A-effect) consists in representing the incidents of real life on the stage in such a way that it's their very causality that is particularly in evidence and occupies the audience. Emotions are also produced by this art form and it is precisely the mastering of reality which, made possible by these demonstrations, induces emotions in the audience. The A-effect is an old aesthetic device, familiar from comedy, certain branches of folk-art and the practices of the Asiatic Theatre.

[2] One must not search for something especially profound and mysterious in this. The actor needs to do nothing more than is done by other people when they describe something with the intention of making it manageable. It is solely a method of focusing interest on what is to be described, of making it interesting. Certain things one takes for granted become in this way not so self-evident—admittedly only so that they may now become understandable.

Effekt is intended *simply* to alienate the audience and break an illusion; at the same time it shows Brecht insisting once more on the interrelationship of reason and feeling:

> der schauspieler greid verwendet anstatt 'verfremden' immer 'objektivieren' und meint damit darstellungen ohne gefühl. das gibt mir gelegenheit, einen wohl leicht möglichen irrtum zu klären . . . bei den panoramagemälden der jahrmärkte (<nero betrachtet den brand roms>, <erschiessung des anarchisten ferner>, < das erdbeben von lissabon>) ist der v-effekt reines gefühl. in dem aristotelischen theater ist die einfühlung auch eine geistige, das nichtaristotelische theater benutzt auch gefühlsmassige kritik.[1]   (*AJ*, p. 192)

[1] instead of 'make strange' the actor greid always uses the word 'objectify' and means by this presentations without feeling. this gives me the opportunity to explain an error that might easily arise . . . in the case of the panorama paintings of the fairgrounds (<nero watching rome burning> <the shooting of the anarchist ferner>, <the lisbon earthquake>) the a-effect is pure feeling. in the aristotelian theatre the empathy is also an intellectual one. the non-aristotelian theatre also uses an emotional critical attitude.

8

The Poetry

In a letter to Alfred Döblin, written in 1928, Brecht declined the latter's invitation to appear at a poetry reading with the following comment:

> ... (ich) habe ... schwere Hemmungen, da man mir meine Lyrik immer so schwer ankreidet, dass mir seit langem schon jeder Reim im Hals stecken bleibt! Meine Lyrik ist nämlich das schlagendste Argument gegen meine Dramen! Alle sagen sofort, befreit aufatmend, mein Vater hätte mich eben Lyriker und nicht Dramatiker werden lassen sollen![1] (*ÜL*, pp. 57–8)

The wry tone of these remarks shows they need to be taken with some scepticism. Nevertheless, the final sentence, for all its flippancy, does raise the important question of the relationship between Brecht the poet and Brecht the dramatist.

It is on his work in the theatre that Brecht's reputation is based, to the comparative neglect of his importance as a poet. There is little to be gained from any comparative evaluation in which plus and minus points are awarded in turn to the poetry and the drama. But to overlook Brecht's poetic gifts and the poetic strain which runs through his drama can lead to a dangerously undifferentiated view of his work. John Willett was the first to make a special case for a suitably adjusted approach. In his article 'The Poet Beneath The Skin' he presses the case for Brecht the poet:

> At the end of it all we come back to the poet, because you

[1] (I) have serious reservations, since my poetry is laid so heavily to my account that for a long time now every rhyme has been sticking in my gullet: the fact is, my lyric poetry is the strongest argument against my plays! Everybody immediately says, with a sigh of relief, that my father should have put me into poetry and not play-writing!

cannot appreciate the playwright Brecht, or even perhaps the theatrical director, let alone the theoretician, without realizing that he was a poet first, last, and all the time.

(*Brecht Heute 2*, p. 88)

And although Hannah Arendt, as far back as 1950, had said 'Ich habe keinen Zweifel daran, dass Bertolt Brecht der grösste lebende deutsche Lyriker ist' (I have no doubt that Bertolt Brecht is the greatest living German lyric poet), Brecht's poetic *oeuvre* remains largely unknown. There is no full-scale critical survey of it, and, compared with the studies of the dramas, surprisingly few interpretations of individual poems. And yet even a cursory acquaintance with the poetry shows the reader that here is a writer who stands head and shoulders above other twentieth-century German poets. An impressive range of themes, supreme technical skill, the sharp ear for speech rhythms, and a highly individual and unmistakable tone of voice—these are the characteristics of Brecht's verse.

Early Poems

Yet his beginnings were far from auspicious. The poetry from 1913–15, dealing mostly with the war, is forceful but hardly remarkable for its individuality. It uses the free rhythms of Whitman and the Expressionists, together with a large dose of 'Pathos': and although poems like 'Der Tsingtausoldat' (The Tsingtau Soldier) (*GW 8*, pp. 11–12) are frequently cited as fine instances of the young Brecht's insight into the brutalities of the war they seem, when compared with the work of Wilfred Owen or Siegfried Sassoon, self-conscious and weighed down with leaden hyperbole. Furthermore, the poems and articles he was writing for the Augsburg papers in 1914–15 (and which have just been printed) hardly confirm the picture of Brecht as the young rebel violently opposed to the war and all its horrors. While the language is over-blown and laden with adjectives, the subjects are notable for their conventionality—ranging from praise of the Kaiser, through self-consciously melancholic thoughts on the sinking of the *Emden* and her drowned

crew, to an appallingly inept and juvenile prose-ballad on a
Fahnenjunker (officer cadet) who is the embodiment of the
troops' ideas and wishes. It is only in 1916 with the poems
'Tanzballade' (Dance-ballad) and 'Soldatengrab' (Soldier's
Grave) that Brecht seems to have found a form and style which
are to prove more productive and congenial. Dating from the
same year is the poem 'Das Lied von der Eisenbahntruppe von
Fort Donald' (The Song of the Fort Donald Railroad Gang),
a vivid account of a gang of railway men striking a path through
the American wilderness before being engulfed by a forest that
becomes a lake! With this, the young poet sets out on a trail
which is to lead through the jungles of South America, across
the seven seas, down streams and rivers and into dark forests
which are the haunts and final resting-places of those soldiers
of fortune, free-booters, outlaws and murderers who are the
heroes of his early work. If it all sounds like jolly escapist
literature, nothing could be further from the truth. The figures
as well as the themes of the poetry are part of a definite
literary tradition, running back through Kipling and Wedekind
to Rimbaud and Whitman and ultimately to the father of all
poètes maudits, François Villon.

Allied to this fascination for such elemental themes as love,
death, murder, the outsider and nature, and the absence of God
is his preference for the traditional popular poetic forms, the
ballad and *Volkslied* (folk song), and the *Moritat*. The style
and form of the war poetry were far more in keeping with the
acceptable modern idiom of the time than are the rhymed
ballads and songs to which he now turned. As he was later to
confess (forgetting, perhaps conveniently, the earlier aberra-
tions):

> Ich begann z.B. mit den einfachsten, gewöhnlichsten
> Arten der Lyrik, dem Bänkelsang und der Ballade, For-
> men, welche von den besseren Dichtern schon längst
> nicht mehr gepflegt wurden.[1]   (*ÜL*, p. 30)

---

[1] I began for example with the simplest, most usual types of lyric poetry,
the *Bänkelsang* and the ballad, forms which for some time had no longer
found favour with the better poets.

Another comment, also from the thirties, makes the same point:

> Die Ballade war eine uralte Form und zu meiner Zeit
> schrieb niemand mehr Balladen, der etwas auf sich hielt.
> Später bin ich in der Lyrik zu anderen Formen überge-
> gangen, weniger alten, aber ich bin mitunter zurück-
> gekehrt und habe sogar Kopien alter Meister gemacht,
> Villon und Kipling übertragen.[1]   (ibid., p. 14)

His mastery of the ballad is seen at its best in poems like the
'Ballade von den Seeräubern' (Ballad of the Pirates) (*GW 8*,
pp. 224–8) with its pirates looting, lusting and roaring out their
song and the poem's refrain as the storm swallows them up:

> O Himmel, strahlender Azur!
> Enormer Wind, die Segel bläh!
> Lasst Wind und Himmel fahren! Nur
> Lasst uns um Sankt Marie die See![2]

The language and the movement of the verse vividly reflect
their changing moods. As they carouse the nights away after
the day's exertions, the poem's tempo drops accordingly. It is
rather like a dance of death in which the participants, instead
of whirling on in an ever-wilder frenzy, become noticeably more
apathetic and jaded as the poem progresses, until in the last
stanza, they rouse themselves in a final gesture of defiance.
The opening stanza, with its jostling descriptive phrases used
as abrupt exclamations is the most dynamic of all: by stanza
eight, the pirates are *müd* (tired), *satt* (fed up), the ship's motion
almost imperceptible:

> Mag Mond und zugleich Sonne scheinen:
> Man hat Gesang und Messer satt.
> Die hellen Sternennächte schaukeln

---

[1] The ballad was an age-old form and in my time nobody with any opinion of himself wrote ballads any longer. Later I changed to other forms,
ones not so old, but from time to time I have gone back and have even
made copies of old masters, translated Villon and Kipling.

[2] Oh heavenly sky of radiant blue!
Enormous wind, let the sails blow free!
The wind and sky can go to the devil! Just
Let us keep, oh Sweet Marie, the sea!

Sie mit Musik in süsse Ruh
Und mit geblähten Segeln gaukeln
Sie unbekannten Meeren zu.[1]

The mood of stanzas nine and ten is similarly—if ominously—tranquil, the tone impassive and unruffled. Images of calm and gentleness ('in aller Stille' (in complete tranquillity), 'das milde Licht' (the mild light)) contrast sharply with the brutal directness of the statement that the sea has now had enough of them. The winds *schieben* (push) and *fächeln* (fan) the pirates' vessel, the evening smiles benignly, and the storm suddenly shatters this deceptively idyllic seascape and is just as suddenly gone, leaving behind the echo of their defiant shanty.

This patterning of the dynamic and the static, and the way it conditions a poem's structure and atmosphere are recurrent features of the early poetry. Brecht makes masterly use of this effect in the great 'Ballade vom Mazeppa' (*GW 8*, pp. 233–5), his own distinctive re-interpretation of the historical brigand's ride, which had also been the subject of poems by Byron and Victor Hugo. The Romantics have their Cossack rebel rescued when his horse collapses. Brecht's horse rushes the bound hero to a death which is drawn out over three days: time seems to stand still, the sky flashes by overhead, never-ending, as if in some nightmarish dream sequence where Mazeppa somehow hovers suspended between the rushing sky and the panting, demented horse. The final stanza, with its perfectly judged diminuendo and gradual arresting of the rhythm is a good instance of Brecht's feel for tonal counterpoint. The mood of the lines is calm, almost reflective after the hectic preceding stanzas: but the tone is controlled and assertive reflecting the poet's conviction—which he shares with his pirates and adventurers—that death is not the negation of vitality but its logical and acceptable complement:

[1] The moon and sun may shine together:
  But soon one's had enough of songs and knives.
  The bright-lit starry nights will rock them
  With sound of music to gentle rest
  And with the sails all swelling they'll
  Flit across unknown, uncharted seas.

Drei Tage lang ritt er durch Abend und Morgen
Bis er alt genug war, dass er nicht mehr litt
Als er gerettet ins grosse Geborgen
Todmüd in die ewige Ruhe einritt.[1]

Such moments are, in the words of Hannah Arendt '. . . among
the truly immortal lines of German poetry' (*NY*, p. 97).

Popular Forms and Private Meanings

Brecht had a sure sense of the musicality of poetry, unrivalled
in German verse since Heine. Willett accurately sums up this
gift when he writes '. . . poetically . . . he seemed to think in
near-musical terms' (p. 125). Music is an essential element in
Brecht's work—nowhere more so than in these early poems,
many of which, after the example of Wedekind, were intended
to be sung to guitar accompaniment. It was not a case of writing the text and then coming up with a tune: the two were
mutually dependent, as Brecht himself pointed out: 'In der
Lyrik habe ich mit Liedern zur Guitarre angefangen und die
Verse zugleich mit der Musik entworfen'[2] (*ÜL*, p. 14). In fact,
in some cases, the poem's rhythm was predetermined by the
pulse of the melody. The musical settings included in the
Hauspostille of 1927 are but a small sample of Brecht's own
compositions: though not formally trained, he had absorbed
the rhythms, phrasing and melodic line of forms as diverse
as the chorale, hymn, popular song and *Bänkelsang* (popular
ballad), and drew on them extensively for his own poetry.
It was the *Hauspostille* which introduced him to the public as
the most accomplished and distinctive poet of traditional forms
since Heine. Yet, in spite of the fact that he chooses the ballad
and *Lied* for most of the poems, there is an odd combination
of the public and private voice in many of them. The rhymed
ballad can be seen as the most accessible and public of poetic

[1] For three long days he rode through evening and morning
Till he was old enough to suffer no more
And so received into the great realm of redemption
He rode tired unto death to his eternal rest.
[2] In the field of the lyric I began with songs with guitar accompaniment
and drafted the lines at the same time as the music.

forms, assuming, as it does, a relatively straightforward relationship between poet and audience, and presenting its subject-matter through the combination of simple narrative and dramatic action. But poems such as 'Historie vom verliebten Schwein Malchus' (Little history of Malchus, the pig that fell in love) (*GW 8*, pp. 201–5) or the 'Ballade von den Geheimnissen jedweden Mannes' (Ballad of the secrets of any man in the world) (ibid., pp. 218–19) are notable more for their mood than for their intelligibility. Such meaning as there is in these poems is so puzzling and allusive as to be well-nigh incomprehensible even to those familiar with Brecht's world of decay, brutality and distorted identity. The justification for the presence of such poems in a collection which, on the whole, contrasts sharply with the hermetic poetry of a George or Rilke, can be found in the title itself. It is *Bertolt Brechts Hauspostille*, not *Die Hauspostille*—a title which emphasizes both the usability of the selection as well as its personal relevance. And Brecht's 'Anleitung zum Gebrauch der einzelnen Lektionen' (Instructions for the use of the individual lessons) combines private whimsy and quirky in-jokes with relatively straightforward instructions to the general reader on how he should 'use' (not 'read' or 'immerse himself in') the poems.

When this is borne in mind, Brecht's remarks in an interview from 1926 can be seen to apply not only to that mass of personal and private poems not included in the *Hauspostille*, but also to the collection itself:

> Meine Lyrik hat mehr privaten Charakter . . . Im Drama hingegen gebe ich nicht meine private Stimmung, sondern gleichsam die Stimmung der Welt. Mit andern Worten: eine objektiv angeschaute Sache, das Gegenteil von Stimmung im gewöhnlichen und poetischen Sinn.[1]
>
> (*SzT 2*, p. 287)

The definition of his dramatic style might have seemed exact

---

[1] My lyric poetry has more of a private character . . . In the drama on the other hand I do not offer my private mood, but the mood of the world, so to speak. In other words: a matter objectively viewed, the opposite of mood in the usual and poetic sense.

to the author in 1926 when he was moving away from the formalism and atmospheric imagery of the early plays. Yet it is wildly inaccurate when referred back to *Im Dickicht der Städte* and just as inappropriate when referred forward to plays like *Der gute Mensch von Sezuan* or *Kreidekreis*. But Brecht was, in part, reacting against the familiar critical fondness for consigning a writer's work to clearly labelled pigeonholes.

The Role of the Poet: Function and 'Beauty' in Brecht's Poetics

In the *Anleitung* (Introduction) to the *Hauspostille* Brecht makes a not altogether convincing attempt to emphasize the *Gebrauchswert* (functional value) of the poetry: the chronicles should be read during times of rainstorms, snowfalls, bankruptcies, etc., the *Mahagonnygesänge* during the hours of wealth, awareness of the desires of the flesh and presumption. Nevertheless, the collection could hardly be considered an example of *Gebrauchslyrik* (functional verse) in the most commonly accepted sense. The next collection *Lieder Gedichte Chöre* (Songs Poems Choruses), published in Paris in 1934, brings together a number of the most effective political poems, choruses and marching songs from the years which saw Brecht becoming more involved in politics, the situation in Germany and Marxist philosophy. The exuberance and colourful language of the *Hauspostille* are here replaced by a more sober, consciously manipulated style. Such a development was a logical result of the study of Marxism: the tone of the voice is now that of the poet on the public platform. The domestic breviary has become a manual of and for the times. The strengths and weaknesses of such poems should be viewed not only in relation to the earlier verse, but also in terms of Brecht's aims, his deliberate departure from a view of poetry as an expression of feelings or 'mood':

> Wenn man die Lyrik als Ausdruck bezeichnet, muss man wissen, dass eine solche Bezeichnung einseitig ist. Da drücken sich Individuen aus, da drücken sich Klassen aus,

da haben Zeitalter ihren Ausdruck gefunden und Leiden-
schaften . . .[1]   (*ÜL*, p. 27)

The political songs, the anti-Hitler satires, and the marching
choruses should not be compared with, for instance, Auden's
'Spain 1937' or Yeats' 'Easter 1916' and 'September 1913':
rather are their counterparts the posters and photo-montages
of John Heartfield, songs like the Mayakovsky–Eisler 'Rote
Kolonne' (Red Column), or 'Die Moorsoldaten' (The bog
soldiers). Furthermore, any judgement of their effectiveness
cannot be based simply on a reading of the printed text. Poems
like the 'Einheitsfrontlied' (Song of the United Front) (*GW*
9, pp. 652–3) derive their impetus and conviction from Eisler's
music as much as from Brecht's words—more so, in fact. A
stirring and lively tune will not only compensate for any weaknesses in the text, it is also the surest way of making the text
itself more memorable. Such songs were written with a definite
audience in mind, and arose from an actual historical need.
As Eisler put it, speaking also of the 'Solidaritätslied' (Song
of Solidarity):

> . . . ohne Praxis geht dieses Genre nicht. Also als Kunst-
> leistung für den Schreibtisch oder für ein paar Versamm-
> lungen geht das Genre nicht . . . So ähnlich . . . —ich
> glaube Marx sagt das irgendwo oder Engels—ist das mit
> den Liedern der Chartisten, die einen historischen Sinn
> hatten und in einer gewissen Periode überholt wurden . . .
> Das kann man nur schreiben, wenn man eine ganz be-
> stimmte konkrete gesellschaftliche Situation vorfindet.[2]
>
> (*Fragen Sie mehr über Brecht*, p. 56)

[1] When one defines lyric poetry as expression, one needs to know that
such a definition is one-sided. Individuals express themselves, classes express themselves, centuries have found their expression and passions as
well . . .

[2] . . . without the realization in practice this genre can't work. I mean,
as an artistic performance for the writing desk or for a few gatherings the
genre won't work. It's the same sort of thing—I think Marx says that
somewhere, or Engels—with the songs of the Chartists, which had an
historical meaning and were obsolete within a certain period of time . . .
That sort of thing can only be written if one finds a quite definite concrete
social situation to hand.

In the thirties, Brecht's poetry shows him becoming more concerned with the question of the poet's audience, the function of poetry and the need to find a new style and idiom in which he could address himself to the problems of the times. He had always been opposed to that type of verse which speaks in opaque riddles to an audience of credulous initiates. 'Pure lyrical utterances' were to him anathema:

> Sie entfernen sich einfach zu weit von der ursprünglichen Geste der Mitteilung eines Gedankens oder einer auch für Fremde vorteilhaften Empfindung. Alle grossen Gedichte haben den Wert von Dokumenten. In ihnen ist die Sprechweise des Verfassers enthalten, eines wichtigen Menschen.[1] (*ÜL*, p. 8)

The poet must realize that he is speaking for and to an audience —and this does not entail talking down to it. The case for this view of the relationship betwen the artist and his public is well put, in a different context, by Graham Greene:

> I doubt if the best work has ever been produced in complete independence of a public . . . Popular *taste* makes a thoroughly bad dictator, but the awareness of an audience is an essential discipline for the artist.
> (*The Pleasure Dome*, p. 40)

This attitude does not restrict the artist to producing mere journalism; nor did Brecht see it as meaning that poetry had to eschew the personal and reflective. What he abhorred was that poetry of self-communion, so common in German literature, where 'nomen est omen': that is, a spiritual, secular or metaphysical ritual in which the poet is celebrant, communicant and congregation rolled into one, while the reader stands (or preferably kneels) without the walls of the hallowed sanctuary.

Even in his most extreme phase in the late twenties, Brecht

---

[1] They simply move too far away from the original gesture of communicating a thought or affording a sensation which even strangers would find profitable. All great poems have the value of documents. In them is contained the manner of speaking of the writer himself—an important human being.

was not prepared to insist on *Nützlichkeit* (usefulness) as the sole criterion for a successful poem. In 1927 he had refused to award a prize in a poetry competition he had been asked to judge: and the follow-up essay in which he sets out in more detail his views on lyric poetry is entitled 'Weder nützlich noch schön' (neither useful nor beautiful). It is, at first sight, odd to find Brecht of all people using this latter term, so beloved of German writers on aesthetics since Schiller. Yet it is not arbitrarily chosen, for, over the following years, he develops a poetic which is based on the awareness of the demands of *prodesse* (to be useful) and *delectare* (to please). There is no place in the twentieth-century poet's work for a one-sided view either of life or of art. Hence, Brecht invariably proposes a dual standard for the assessment of a work and strives for a poetry which will accommodate the dialectical interplay of various opposing elements. The poet should never shun *Verstand* (the intellect) in favour of *Gefühl* (the emotions)—nor, indeed, vice versa:

> Einige Lyriker, besonders Anfänger, scheinen, wenn sie sich in Stimmung fühlen, Furcht zu haben, aus dem Verstand Kommendes könne die Stimmung verscheuchen ... Wie man aus den Werkstattenberichten grosser Lyriker weiss, handelt es sich bei ihren Stimmungen keineswegs um so oberflächliche, labile, leicht verfliegende Stimmungen, dass umsichtiges, ja nüchternes Nachdenken stören könnte. Die gewisse Beschwingtheit und Erregtheit ist der Nüchternheit keineswegs direkt entgegengesetzt ... Ist das lyrische Vorhaben ein glückliches, dann arbeiten Gefühl und Verstand völlig im Einklang.[1]
>
> (*ÜL*, p. 29)

[1] Some lyric poets—especially beginners—seem, when they feel themselves in the mood, to be afraid that anything which comes from the rational faculties might dispel the mood ... As one knows from the 'workshop reports' of great poets there is no question at all—in the case of their moods—of moods so superficial, labile and easily evaporating that discreet or even sober reflection might prove a disturbance. That certain verve and the excitement are by no means directly opposed to sobriety ... If the poetic enterprise is a felicitous one, then feeling and reason can work together in complete harmony.

Thus, he can take issue with Arthur Waley because the latter cannot see that there is no distinction between *Didaktik* (didacticism) and *Amüsement* (amusement) (*ÜL*, p. 48): or speaking of a passable political poem by Fritz Brügel, he can sum up his objections as follows: 'Es ist ziemlich gleichgültig, ob man sagt, es habe keine Kraft, weil es der Logik mangelt, oder, es mangle der Logik, weit es keine Kraft habe'[1] (*ÜL*, p. 24). At first sight, this sort of remark merely seems like a neat paradox: yet, when taken together with Brecht's precise objections to the poem, it is full of common sense. Images which have a taut logic of their own will lend strength and sinew to the poem's language and its argument; while lame diction and limp metaphors are signs of inadequacy in the poet's propositions.

This dialectical view of reality and the work of art, and the need for a type of poetry which will accommodate both the pressing questions of the age as well as Wordsworth's 'lovely apparition sent to be a moment's ornament' provide the thematic and structural basis for Brecht's poetry from 1935 onwards. He would concur with the view of the poet Dr Johnson expresses through the character of Imlac in *Rasselas*:

> To a poet nothing can be useless. Whatever is beautiful, and whatever is dreadful, must be familiar to his imagination . . . The business of a poet . . . is to examine, not the individual, but the species; to remark general properties and large appearances . . . the knowledge of nature is only half the task . . . he must be acquainted likewise with all the modes of life.

The poet must endeavour to come to terms with the problems of his time: on the other hand, he must also find in his work a place for those themes and experiences which reflect his conviction that a 'Gespräch über Bäume' (conversation about trees), even though it may seem a crime, is nevertheless an essential part of the human and artistic consciousness. Although some poems taken in isolation may appear to be advocating a

---

[1] It is fairly immaterial whether one says it has no force because it lacks logic, or it lacks logic because it has no force.

type of poetry which has no place for the traditional lyric mode, its themes and motifs, Brecht was artist enough to introduce by the back door the very thing he seems to be banishing. This technique is well illustrated by the following two poems:

> Ausschliesslich wegen der zunehmenden Unordnung
> In unseren Städten des Klassenkampfs
> Haben etliche von uns in diesen Jahren beschlossen
> Nicht mehr zu reden von Hafenstädten, Schnee auf den
>   Dächern, Frauen
> Geruch reifer Äpfel im Keller, Empfindungen des Fleisches
> All dem, was den Menschen rund macht und menschlich
> Sondern zu reden nur mehr von der Unordnung
> Also einseitig zu werden, dürr, verstrickt in die Geschäfte
> Der Politik und das trockene 'unwürdige' Vokabular
> Der dialektischen Ökonomie
> Damit nicht dieses furchtbare gedrängte Zusammensein
> Von Schneefällen (sie sind nicht nur kalt, wir wissen's)
> Ausbeutung, verlocktem Fleisch und Klassenjustiz eine
>   Billigung
> So vielseitiger Welt in uns erzeuge, Lust an
> Den Widersprüchen solch blutigen Lebens
> Ihr versteht.[1]   (*GW 9*, p. 519)

---

[1] Solely because of the increasing disorder
In our cities of class struggle
Some of us have in the course of these years decided
To speak no more of seaports, snow on the roofs, women,
The smell of ripe apples in the cellars, sensations of the flesh, of
All that makes a man fully rounded and human,
But to speak from now on only of the disorder
That is, to become one-sided, arid, enmeshed in the business
Of politics and the dry 'unworthy' vocabulary
Of dialectical economics
So that this fearful cramped existence side by side
Of snowfalls (they're not merely cold, we know)
Exploitation, lured flesh and class-justice, should not engender
Approval in us of a world so many-sided; delight in
The contradictions of such a cruel life
You understand.

In finsteren Zeiten

Man wird nicht sagen: Als da der Nussbaum sich im Wind
    schüttelte
Sondern: Als da der Anstreicher die Arbeiter niedertrat.
Man wird nicht sagen: Als das Kind den flachen Kiesel
    über die Stromschnelle springen liess
Sondern: Als da die grossen Kriege vorbereitet wurden.
Man wird nicht sagen: Als da die Frau ins Zimmer kam
Sondern: Als da die grossen Mächte sich gegen die
    Arbeiter verbündeten.
Aber man wird nicht sagen: Die Zeiten waren finster
Sondern: Warum haben ihre Dichter geschwiegen?[1]

                                        (*GW 9*, p. 587)

Such themes called also for new styles and forms more appropriate to them: they could not be encompassed within the
traditional forms with their regular rhyme and metre. Examples
of what he later came to describe as 'reimlose Lyrik mit unregelmässigen Rhythmen' (rhymeless verse with irregular
rhythms) occur among the poetry of the twenties, but the style
reaches maturity in the poetry of the thirties and forties. Brecht
was well aware of what he was doing: the move away from
regular forms was no mere fondness for experimentation or
formalism:

Ich zog mich zurück auf den freien Vers, als der Reim nicht
    mehr ausreichte für das, was zu sagen war.[2]

                                        (*ÜL*, p. 30)

Sehr regelmässige Rhythmen hatten auf mich eine mir

---

[1]   *In Dark Times*
    They won't say: when the walnut tree shook in the wind
    But: when the house-painter crushed the workers.
    They won't say: when the child skimmed the flat stone across the
        rapids
    But: when the great wars were being prepared for.
    They won't say: when the woman came into the room
    But: when the great powers joined forces against the workers.
    Yet they won't say: the times were dark
    But: why did their poets stay silent?
[2] I went back to free verse when rhyme no longer sufficed for what was
to be said.

unangenehme einlullende, einschläfernde Wirkung . . .
Ausserdem war die Sprechweise des Alltags in so glatten
Rhythmen nicht unterzubringen, es sei denn ironisch.
Und der nüchterne Ausdruck schien mir keineswegs so
unvereinbar mit dem Gedicht, wie oft behauptet wurde . . .
Bei unregelmässigen Rhythmen bekamen die Gedanken
eher die ihnen entsprechenden eigenen emotionellen For-
men . . . Für einige der sozialen Funktionen, welche die
Lyrik hat, konnten da neue Wege beschritten werden.[1]

(ibid., p. 88)

The large number of nature poems, love sonnets and personal reflections on exile and objects which meant much to him
give the lie to any picture of Brecht as a latter-day Verlaine,
substituting *lyrisme* (lyricism) for *éloquence* (rhetoric) and
crying 'Prends le lyrisme et tords-lui son cou!' (take lyricism
and wring its neck). He does not develop a consistent aesthetic
which places the lyric mode a poor second to political and
historical realities. In the mature poetry he combines images
from both areas, setting them one against the other, allowing
them to relate and interact within the poem, and thereby poses
questions for which both he and the reader must seek an answer.
The poetry from the years in Scandinavia and the U.S.A. can
be seen as an unceasing attempt to describe and analyse that
mood he finds so difficult to understand when he writes, in a
diary entry for September 1940:

es wäre unglaublich schwierig, den gemütstand aus-
zudrücken, in dem ich am radio und in den schlechten
finnisch-schwedischen, zeitungen der schlacht um england
folge und dann den *Puntila* schreibe. dieses geistige phäno-
men erklärt gleichermassen, dass solche kriege sein
können und dass immer noch literarische arbeiten ange-
fertigt werden können. der puntila geht mich fast nichts
an, der krieg alles; über den puntila kann ich fast alles
schreiben, über den krieg nichts. ich meine nicht nur

[1] Very regular rhythms had an unpleasant, lulling, soporific effect on me
. . . Besides, it was not possible to accommodate the tenor of everyday
speech to such smooth rhythms, except ironically. And a sober mode of
expression struck me as far from irreconcilable with poetry, as was often
asserted . . . With the use of irregular rhythms, thoughts acquired their
own emotional forms more in keeping with them . . . New paths could
thus be pursued for some of the social functions that lyric poetry does have.

'darf', ich meine auch wirklich 'kann'. es ist interessant,
wie weit die literatur, als praxis, wegverlegt ist von den
zentren der alles entscheidenden geschehnisse.[1]

(*AJ*, p. 171)

The Move Towards a More Concise Style

Although it may be felt that Brecht had said all he had to say
on his own position by 1940 in such large-scale works as the
Chroniken from the *Svendborger Gedichte* (Svendborg Poems),
and poems like 'An die Nachgeborenen' (To Posterity) and 'Die
Literatur wird durchforscht werden' (Literature will be scrutin-
ized), the subsequent years in America and Berlin do not indi-
cate any decline in his poetic gifts. The poetry becomes more
intimate and that vein of subdued eloquence which had become
the hallmark of the exile verse becomes even more restrained.
Prompted by his work on the translation—from the English
of Arthur Waley—of some Chinese poems, he had begun by
the end of the thirties to develop a deliberate sparseness of
imagery. Though he never sought to write either strict 'haiku'
or 'tanka' verse, the affinities with these forms are obvious from
poems such as 'Rückkehr' (Return) (*GW 10*, p. 858) or 'Tages-
anbruch' (The Break of Day) (ibid., p. 868):

> Nicht umsonst
> Wird der Anbruch jeden neuen Tages
> Eingeleitet durch das Krähen des Hahns
> Anzeigend seit alters
> Einen Verrat.[2]

[1] it would be incredibly difficult to describe the state of mind in which i'm
following the battle of britain on the radio and in the poor finnish–swedish
newspapers, and then writing *puntila*. this mental phenomenon likewise
accounts for the fact that such wars can happen and that literary works
can still go on being produced. *puntila* concerns me hardly at all, while the
war really does; i can write almost everything on *puntila*, and on the war,
nothing. i don't only mean 'may', i really also do mean 'can'. it is interesting
ust how far literature, as practice, is removed from the centres of the
events that decide everything.

[2] Not for nothing
Is the dawning of each new day
Heralded by the crowing of the cock
Ever the announcement of
A betrayal.

This small-scale, carefully wrought poetry reaches its cul-
mination in the cycle *Buckower Elegien*, written in 1953; it takes
its title from the suburb of Berlin where Brecht had a small
cottage. The tone of these poems, as indeed of the majority of
poems from the years 1949–56 is elegiac, subdued, often bord-
ering on resignation. But the poems are saved from sliding
into limp apathy by Brecht's controlled language and the
direct, matter-of-fact style. Each one is a poetic thought distilled
to its essence, an invitation to the reader not to yield passively
to their elegiac mood but to respond actively and critically to
the picture the poet presents. It is a poetry of subtle brush-
strokes and elliptical statements which are at times puzzling
and enigmatic, but never deliberately obscurantist. These are,
in many respects, among the most personal of all Brecht's
poems, and cannot be divorced from his own situation as artist
and Marxist in the G.D.R. 'Die Kelle' (The Trowel), for example
(which was not included in the cycle when it first appeared)
chooses an everyday metaphor to comment on the artist's
position:

> Im Traum stand ich auf einem Bau. Ich war
> Ein Maurer. In der Hand
> Hielt ich eine Kelle. Aber als ich mich bückte
> Nach dem Mörtel, fiel ein Schuss
> Der riss mir von meiner Kelle
> Das halbe Eisen.[1]   (*GW 10*, p. 1015)

The reader is left reflecting not only on the scene, but also on
the possible outcome: not only on how *der Maurer* (the bricklayer) *might* have reacted, but how he *ought* to react. In this
connection, the title is important: it is not 'Der Maurer', but
'Die Kelle'; the tool is partly shattered, but only partly, and
he must make do with it. No situation, no society is perfect:
man and artist must make the best of both, not in a spirit of

[1] In a dream I stood on a building site. I was
A bricklayer. In my hand
I held a trowel. But as I bent down
For the mortar, a shot rang out
That tore from my trowel
Half the iron.

submissive acceptance but with an active awareness that in-
adequacies and injustices can and must be remedied. A prosaic
and common-place idea, perhaps: but it lies at the heart of
Brecht's view of the world.

More than the drama, more than the theoretical and political
writings, Brecht's poetry time and again bears witness to his

> overriding assumption that literature, world events, the
> theatre, domestic objects, human behaviour and even the
> landscape all hang together ... his sense that his own
> function was to work and work in order to show how they
> did so, thus helping us all to understand the world in
> which we live.   ('Brecht in Exile')

It is this quality, together with the unequalled command of
language—in turn supple and monumental, precise and sug-
gestive, luminous and unadorned—that sets Brecht apart as
one of the greatest European poets. Never one to hide his light
under a bushel—though never addicted to an extravagant
parading of personality—he was frequently given to assessing
his own performance and the nature of his achievement. Holding wisely to the principle that humility is based on truth, he had
years before, in the prose work *Me-Ti*, set down a résumé of
his contribution to literature. It is worth quoting:

> Der Dichter Kin-jeh [a pen-name for Brecht himself] darf
> für sich das Verdienst in Anspruch nehmen, die Sprache
> der Literatur erneuert zu haben. Er fand zwei Sprach-
> weisen vor: Eine stilisierte, welche gespreizt und ge-
> schrieben klang und nirgends im Volk, bei der Erledigung
> der Geschäfte oder bei anderen Angelegenheiten, ge-
> sprochen wurde, und eine überall gesprochene, welche
> eine blosse Imitation des alltäglichen Redens und nicht
> stilisiert war. Er wandte eine Sprachweise an, die zugleich
> stilisiert und natürlich war. Die erreichte er, indem er auf
> die Haltungen achtete, die den Sätzen zugrunde liegen:
> Er brachte nur Haltungen in Sätze und liess durch die
> Sätze die Haltungen immer durchscheinen. Eine solche
> Sprache nannte er gestisch, weil sie nur ein Ausdruck für
> die Gesten der Menschen war. Man kann seine Sätze am
> besten lesen, wenn man dabei gewisse körperliche Bewe-

gungen vollführt, die dazu passen . . . Oft kommen inner-
halb eines bestimmten Gestus (wie Trauer) noch viele
andere Gesten vor (wie Allezuzeugenanrufen, Sich-
zurückhalten, Ungerechtwerden usw). Der Dichter Kin
erkannte die Sprache als ein Werkzeug des Handelns und
wusste, dass einer auch dann mit andern spricht, wenn er
mit sich spricht.[1]   (*GW 12*, pp. 458–9)

[1] The writer Kin-jeh can claim on his own behalf that he renewed the
language of literature. He found available two types of language: a stylized
one which sounded affected and written and was never spoken by people,
whether they were conducting business transactions or any other matters;
and one spoken everywhere, which was a mere imitation of everyday
speech and was not stylized. He made use of a type of language which
was at the same time stylized and natural. He achieved this by paying
attention to the attitudes underlying sentences: he only incorporated
attitudes into sentences and always saw that the attitudes were visible
through the sentences. To this kind of language he gave the name 'gestic',
since it was just an expression of people's gestures. His sentences can best
be read by carrying out at the same time certain physical movements which
seem appropriate . . . Often a particular 'Gestus' (such as sadness) can
encompass many other gestures as well (like calling on others to be witness,
controlling oneself, being unjust, etc.) The writer Kin recognized language
as a tool of action and knew that even when someone is speaking to himself, he is also speaking to others.

Chronological Table

The following table is not in any sense complete; it should be read in conjunction with Chapter One and is intended to provide the student with a summary of the most important dates for Brecht's life and work. It is based on Klaus Völker's *Brecht-Chronik*, and students who require fuller details are referred to this invaluable work.

1898	Born 10 February in Augsburg, Southern Germany.
1900	29 June, birth of brother, Walter.
1904–8	Volksschule.
1908–17	Realgymnasium.
1912	'Das Lied vom Geierbaum' earliest known poem.
1913	Editor with Julius Bingen of student periodical 'Die Ernte'; contributes a number of works, among them 'Der brennende Baum' and assorted notices.
1914	Publication in 'Die Ernte' of the one-act play *Die Bibel*. In August he begins his contributions to the 'Erzähler', the literary section of the *Augsburger Neueste Nachrichten*.
1915	27 January, 'Der Kaiser'—a poem in honour of the birthday of Kaiser Wilhelm II.
	30 June, 'Französische Bauern' appears in the *Münchener-Augsburger Abendzeitung*. Unlike the poem above, this hints at a negative attitude on Brecht's part towards the War.
1916	June, the incident concerning Brecht's sharply critical essay on Horace's tag 'Dulce est et decorum pro patria mori'—he is almost expelled from school.
	13 July, publication of 'Das Lied von der Eisenbahntruppe von Fort Donald'; for this poem, Brecht no longer uses the pseudonym 'Berthold Eugen', but 'Bert Brecht'.
1917	Together with three friends, he passes the so-called 'Notabitur'.
	2 October, enrolment at the University in Munich.
1918	First version of *Baal* completed by mid-June. In latter

half of year at work on project 'Der dicke Mann auf der Schiffschaukel'.

1 October, commencement of his 'military service' in Augsburg; after a period in barracks, he becomes an orderly in a hospital for V.D. patients.

1919   'Spartakus' (later *Trommeln in der Nacht*) completed by 13 February. Working on the revision of *Baal* during the early part of the year.

30 July, birth of son Frank (killed in Russia 13 November 1943), child of Brecht and Paula Banholzer (who appears as 'Bie' in a number of the early poems).

Writes a number of one-acters for the famous Munich comedian Karl Valentin, in whose sketches Brecht himself occasionally appeared as musician.

Meets his first wife Marianne Zoff, actress and singer at the theatre in Augsburg.

At work on a number of projects, among them a biblical drama, short stories and numerous poems.

1920   21 February–13 March, first visit to Berlin.

1 May, death of Brecht's mother.

By July, a third version of *Baal*, with which he was by no means happy, was in the hands of the printers, and Brecht was now waiting for publication. In December, the firm refuses to go ahead with publication, out of fear of a possible court action.

1921   Early in the year at work on 'Galgei', a modified and extended version of 'Der dicke Mann auf der Schiffschaukel'.

11 September from a diary entry (*GW 18*, p. 14) it is clear that Brecht is considering the problem of the 'metropolis as jungle'. This theme appears in the project 'Garga', later re-titled 'Im Dickicht' and finally *Im Dickicht der Städte*.

7 November, second trip to Berlin.

1922   After establishing contacts in Berlin, returns to Munich on 26 April.

29 September, first performance of *Trommeln in der Nacht*. *Baal* published in an edition of eight hundred copies.

3 November, marriage to Marianne Zoff.

13 November, Herbert Ihering announces his decision to award Brecht the Kleist Prize for his first three dramas; a second edition of *Baal* appears.

1923   Together with Karl Valentin, Erich Engel and others, at work on a number of film scripts.

12 March, birth of daugher Hanne.

9 May, first performance of 'Im Dickicht'. Arnolt Bronnen introduces Brecht to Helene Weigel.

In autumn, at work with Lion Feuchtwanger on a version of Marlowe's *Edward II*.

8 December, first performance of *Baal*.

Publication of *Trommeln in der Nacht*, dedicated to 'Bie Banholzer'.

1924   19 March, first performance of *Leben Eduards des Zweiten*.

In September moves to Berlin; together with Carl Zuckmayer, assistant to Max Reinhardt at the Deutsches Theater.

3 November, birth of Stefan, son of Brecht and Helene Weigel. At work on 'Galgei', now re-titled *Mann ist Mann*.

Publication of *Leben Eduards des Zweiten*.

1925   Writes a number of sonnets—his first venture in this form—among them 'Kuh beim Fressen' and 'Die Opiumraucherin'. Completes work on *Mann ist Mann*.

1926   Rewriting of *Baal*, now entitled 'Lebenslauf des Mannes Baal'. It is staged in Berlin on 14 February.

Takes up *Mann ist Mann* once again, this time with the intention of introducing sociological aspects.

25 September, first performance of *Mann ist Mann*.

In the latter half of the year begins his intensive reading of Marx.

11 December, first performance of one-acter *Die Hochzeit*, written some years earlier.

Publication in small private edition of the *Taschenpostille*.

1927   Publication of *Bert Brechts Hauspostille* and *Mann ist Mann*.

Beginning of collaboration with Kurt Weill; first work which results from this is the 'Songspiel' *Mahagonny*, based on the 'Mahagonny-Gesänge' in the *Hauspostille*.

2 November, divorce from Marianne Zoff.

10 December, première of new version of 'Im Dickicht', now entitled *Im Dickicht der Städte*.

1928   Early in the year, Elisabeth Hauptmann translates John Gay's *Beggar's Opera* for Brecht; he receives a commission to rework the libretto for the first production at the opening of the Theater am Schiffbauerdamm.

31 August, first performance of *Die Dreigroschenoper*.

1929   10 April, marriage to Helene Weigel.

Publication of the *Songs der Dreigroschenoper*, which results in the plagiarism accusation from the critic Alfred Kerr.

May, first meeting with Walter Benjamin.

May/June, begins work, together with Elisabeth Hauptmann, Emil Burri, Slatan Dudow and Kurt Weill on the 'Lehrstücke' and *Happy End*.

July, at the Baden-Baden Festival, *Der Flug der Lindberghs* and *Das Badener Lehrstück vom Einverständnis* (the latter with music by Paul Hindemith) receive their first performances.

31 August, first performance of *Happy End*—Brecht is by now strongly critical of the story-line, and wishes to withdraw his name from the list of collaborators, inventing as author 'Dorothy Lane'. Kurt Weill insists that he be mentioned as the author of the songs.

Since 1926, Brecht had been occupying himself with a number of projects for dramas—all of which remained unfinished—among them 'Dan Drew', 'Aus nichts wird nichts', 'Untergang des Egoisten Johannes Fatzer' and 'Joe Fleischhacker'. The fragment 'Der Brotladen' is now written as a result of the work on the latter two projects. All three, together with elements from *Happy End* are later to be fashioned into the full-scale work *Die Heilige Johanna der Schlachthöfe*.

1930   9 March, first performance of the opera *Aufstieg und Fall der Stadt Mahagonny* with music by Kurt Weill.

Working with Hanns Eisler and Slatan Dudow on *Die Massnahme*.

May/June, work on *Die Heilige Johanna der Schlachthöfe* and the 'Lehrstück' *Die Ausnahme und die Regel*.

23 June, first performance of the school opera *Der Jasager*, written in collaboration with Elisabeth Hauptmann and Kurt Weill. After hearing reactions from pupils and teachers to the work, Brecht alters it and writes *Der Neinsager* to balance the moral of *Der Jasager*.

August, submits the film script 'Die Beule' (a reworking of *Die Dreigroschenoper*, on which he had worked with Dudow, Neher and Leo Lania) to the 'Nero Film-Gesellschaft', who object to the line Brecht takes. Brecht sues them, and the resultant 'Dreigroschen-prozess' (*GW 18*, pp. 139–209) arouses much interest and controversy.

18 October, birth of Barbara, daughter of Brecht and Helene Weigel.

10 December, first performance of *Die Massnahme*.

Publication of first two numbers of the *Versuche*.

1931   August, completion of work on the film script for the film *Kuhle Wampe*, written in collaboration with Dudow, Ernst Ottwalt and Hanns Eisler. Work on the film, because of numerous interruptions, lasts until February 1932.

In Autumn, completes work on *Die Mutter*, written in collaboration with Dudow, Eisler, Günther Weisenborn, and based on Gorki's novel.

November, starts work on an adaptation of Shakespeare's *Measure for Measure*.

Together with Elisabeth Hauptmann, Burri and H. Borchardt, finishes the drama *Die Heilige Johanna der Schlachthöfe*.

Publication of numbers three and four of the *Versuche*.

1932   17 January, first public performance of *Die Mutter*.

11 April, broadcast of radio version of *Die Heilige Johanna der Schlachthöfe*.

30 May, first public showing of *Kuhle Wampe* in Berlin though earlier in the month it had already been screened in Moscow.

Finishes work on 'Die Spitzköpfe und die Rundköpfe', a comedy which reworks some of Brecht's material from the *Measure for Measure* adaptation.

Publication of numbers 5, 6 and 7 of the *Versuche*.

1933   28 February, together with his wife and son, leaves Germany for Prague; his daughter follows later.

May, travels to Paris and works with Kurt Weill on the ballet *Die Sieben Todsünden der Kleinbürger*.

7 June, first performance of the ballet.

9 August, buys a house in Skovsbostrand, near Svendborg, on the island of Fyn (Denmark).

September, back in Paris, where Margarete Steffin is preparing the collection *Lieder Gedichte Chöre* for publication.

In Autumn, first meeting with Ruth Berlau, at this time engaged as an actress at the Royal Theatre in Copenhagen.

1934   Writes *Der Dreigroschenroman* and the 'Lehrstück' *Die Horatier und die Kuriatier*, the latter with Margarete Steffin as collaborator.

March, together with Hanns Eisler and Margarete Steffin, Brecht reworks 'Die Spitzköpfe und die Rundköpfe' (which had been ready for printing in number 8 of the *Versuche*) once again. The new version is now entitled *Die Rundköpfe und die Spitzköpfe oder Reich und Reich gesellt sich gern. Ein Greuelmärchen.*

July/August, Brecht correcting the proofs of *Der Dreigroschenroman.*

September, first mention to Benjamin of plans for a drama about Hitler and the *Tui-Roman.*

Publication of *Lieder Gedichte Chöre* (in Paris) and *Der Dreigroschenroman* (in Amsterdam).

1935   Early in the year, travels to Moscow, where he meets Russian and German friends, who are involved with the cultural and political life there. Sees the Chinese actor Mei-Lin-Fang, and, under the impact of the latter's performance, sets down a number of 'Bemerkungen über die chinesische Schauspielkunst', which are published in English in 1936. Reworked, and entitled 'Verfremdungseffekte in der chinesischen Schauspielkunst', the essay was not published in German until 1957.

April, publication of the crucial essay 'Fünf Schwierigkeiten beim Schreiben der Wahrheit'. Conceives the plan for a number of one-act plays, dealing with aspects of life in Hitler's Germany.

October–December, in New York with Hanns Eisler to supervise the American production of *Die Mutter*. Because of arguments and controversy, Brecht and Eisler eventually wash their hands of the whole affair, and spend most of the time going to gangster movies.

1936   Returns to Skovsbostrand; his former teacher and friend Karl Korsch is now there, and the two spend much time together discussing various problems of Marxism and the political situation.

July, appearance in Moscow of first number of the periodical *Das Wort* (editors: Brecht, Willi Bredel and Lion Feuchtwanger). From the very beginning, Brecht's influence on the line the periodical takes on a number of questions is minimal; he eventually takes very little part in the publication of the magazine.

4 November, first performance of *Die Rundköpfe und die Spitzköpfe* (in Danish) in Copenhagen.

1937   Writes further texts for the work he had conceived in

1934, and which had received fresh impetus from the long discussions with Korsch: it is intended as a collection of aphorisms, comments and anecdotes, and is to be called the 'Buch der Wendungen'.

24 March, first version of the play 'Generäle über Bilbao' (later to be entitled *Die Gewehre der Frau Carrar*) written in collaboration with Margarete Steffin.

September, discussions with Erwin Piscator in Paris about a Caesar-drama.

16 October, first performance of *Die Gewehre der Frau Carrar*: (in Paris, performed by émigré actors).

1938　　March, Volumes I and II of the *Gesammelte Werke* published in Prague.

April, the original plan to write a series of five scenes about life in Nazi Germany has grown considerably: there are now twenty-seven scenes to hand which Brecht is drawing on for the cycle *Furcht und Elend des Dritten Reiches*.

7 May, writes the most famous of the exile poems 'Die Legende der Entstehung des Buches Taoteking auf dem Wege des Laotse in die Emigration' (*GW 9*, pp. 660–3).

21 May, first performance of eight scenes from the cycle *Furcht und Elend des Dritten Reiches* under the title '99%'.

July, working on the Caesar-novel, and putting final touches to the collection 'Gedichte im Exil' which is to appear in Volume IV of the *Gesammelte Werke*.

August, the essay 'Weite und Vielfalt der realistischen Schreibweise' conceived as a rejoinder to the position taken up by Georg Lukacs in the debate on Realism and Socialist Realism: it is not published in *Das Wort*, although Brecht had intended it should be.

17 November, Margarete Steffin mentions in a letter to Benjamin that Brecht has begun the actual writing of a drama about Galileo: it was an idea he had been considering for some time.

23 November, the Galileo play finished—a note in Brecht's diary states that it took 'three weeks'.

1939　　Begins serious work on the *Messingkauf* dialogues: the format is suggested to him by Galileo's *Discorsi* which he has been studying for the Galileo drama.

March, using as a starting point a drama-project 'Die Ware Liebe', which he had begun in Berlin, begins work on *Der gute Mensch von Sezuan*.

15 March, Volume III of the *Gesammelte Werke* (containing poems and *Furcht und Elend des Dritten Reiches* and *Leben des Galilei*), which is ready for printing, is seized and destroyed.

23 April, Brecht leaves Denmark for Stockholm. Ruth Berlau remains in Copenhagen to supervise the printing of the *Svendborger Gedichte*.

May, Brecht and his family move into a house on the island of Lidingö.

20 May, Brecht's father dies in Darmstadt.

2 June, completion of the two one-act plays *Dansen* and *Was kostet das Eisen?*

By September, Brecht is making little headway with work on *Der gute Mensch von Sezuan*; on 27 September he turns to *Mutter Courage und ihre Kinder*.

29 October–3 November completes *Mutter Courage und ihre Kinder*.

7 November, according to a diary entry, Brecht has written the radio play *Das Verhör des Lukullus* 'very quickly'.

7 December, Margarete Steffin has given the three completed books of the novel *Die Geschäfte des Herrn Julius Cäsar* to various trade-unionists to read. Encouraged by their comments and reactions Brecht decides to begin work on a fourth book.

1940   17 April, after the invasion of Denmark and Norway by the Nazis, Brecht and his family, together with Margarete Steffin, leave Sweden and sail for Helsinki.

6 May, Brecht has once more taken up work on *Der gute Mensch von Sezuan*.

20 June, *Der gute Mensch von Sezuan*, which has caused him more difficulties than any of his other dramas, is now virtually finished.

7 July, contemplating a drama on the theme 'Jeanne d'Arc 1940'.

27 August, begins work on a 'Volksstück' based on the stories and the comedy *Die Sägespäneprinzessin* by the Finnish author Hella Wuolijoki.

2 September, working on *Puntila*.

19 September, *Puntila* finished.

1 October, the reading of Diderot's *Jacques le Fataliste* prompts Brecht to begin to set down the *Flüchtlingsgespräche*, a project he has been occupied with since his arrival in Finland. He works on them till December.

1941   January, reworking of *Der gute Mensch von Sezuan*.

10 March–12 April, together with Margarete Steffin writes *Der aufhaltsame Aufstieg des Arturo Ui*.

19 April, first performance of *Mutter Courage und ihre Kinder* in Zurich.

15 May, Brecht and his family, together with Margarete Steffin and Ruth Berlau, leave Helsinki for Leningrad, Moscow and Vladivostock.

4 June, on the Trans-Siberia Express word reaches Brecht of the death from tuberculosis of Margarete Steffin in Moscow.

21 July, arrival in Los Angeles. Brecht moves into a house rented for him by friends in Santa Monica.

During the early months Brecht meets a number of old friends from Germany, and establishes contact with various film directors, actors and script-writers.

19 December, nine scenes of 'Jeanne d'Arc 1940' completed.

1942　28 May, Brecht, together with Fritz Lang, has plans for a 'hostage-film' dealing with the assassination of Heydrich in Prague. By the end of July Brecht is working daily on the film with Lang, though he is becoming despondent about the way the original plan is being modified. By the time shooting starts on the film in October/November, he has been forced to watch his script cut and modified to suit the taste of Hollywood: Brecht's suggested title 'Trust the People', is changed to *Hangmen Also Die*.

30 October, Brecht and Feuchtwanger discuss a number of drama-projects: eventually they decide to concentrate on 'Die Stimmen' which is now entitled 'Die Heilige Johanna von Vitry'.

25 November, the projected Saint Joan play is now re-titled *Die Visionen der Simone Machard*.

1943　January, further work with Feuchtwanger on *Die Visionen der Simone Machard*, which for Brecht is relaxation after what he had experienced during the work on the film.

4 February, first performance of *Der gute Mensch von Sezuan* in Zurich.

8 February, Brecht travels to New York to see Ruth Berlau. During his stay he establishes contacts with other German émigrés, and also with W. H. Auden, whom he wishes to persuade to work on an adaptation of Webster's *The Duchess of Malfi*.

26 May, Brecht returns to Santa Monica: on the train he has re-read Hašek's novel *The Good Soldier Schweyk* with a view to possible adaptation and up-dating of the work for the stage. Before commencing work on this project, finishes *Die Gesichte der Simone Machard*.

6 June, has begun intensive work on 'Schweyk'.

24 June, 'Schweyk' virtually complete. At first there are plans for it to be translated into English for a production with Peter Lorre in the title role; by September these plans have come to nothing.

9 September, first performance of *Leben des Galilei* in Zurich.

19 November, travels to New York, where, together with H. R. Hays and Elisabeth Bergner, he continues work on *The Duchess of Malfi*, as well as on a number of other projects.

1944 March, Brecht returns to Santa Monica: there he immediately begins work on *Der kaukasische Kreidekreis*, a sketch for which he had already drawn up in New York.

April, discussions with Charles Laughton, who has read 'Schweyk' in translation and enjoyed it immensely.

June, Brecht suggests Auden, in lieu of Isherwood, as translator for *Der kaukasische Kreidekreis*: the original intention was that the play should be staged on Broadway, and the first version is now ready.

July/August, further work on *Der kaukasische Kreidekreis*.

1 September, the new drafts of the prologue and epilogue to the play are now complete.

From the start of December onwards, systematic work with Charles Laughton on an English version of *Leben des Galilei*.

1945 11 February, since Laughton has film commitments, Brecht decides to begin with a verse adaptation of *The Communist Manifesto*.

14 May, Laughton and Brecht return to work on *Leben des Galilei*.

12 June, première in New York of *The Private Life of the Master-Race*, an English version of *Furcht und Elend des Dritten Reiches*: the English title was suggested some time earlier by Brecht.

July, the adaptation of *The Duchess of Malfi* completed.

2 December, English version of *Leben des Galilei* finished. Brecht tries to interest various producers in the play, but encounters difficulties with agents and finance.

1946	September, first performance of *The Duchess of Malfi* in Boston.
	Paul Dessau, whom Brecht had met in 1943, writes the music for *Mutter Courage und ihre Kinder*.
1947	29 March, Brecht and Helene Weigel obtain an exit and re-enter permit for Switzerland. In the previous year Brecht had written to Caspar Neher in Zurich that he intended to come to Zurich in June 1947.
	31 July, première of *The Life of Galileo* in Beverley Hills.
	30 October, Brecht before the Unamerican Activities Committee.
	31 October, Brecht flies to Paris.
	5 November, travels to Zurich. Meetings with Max Frisch, Carl Zuckmayer, Neher, Werner Bergengruen and other writers, actors and theatre directors.
	21 November, project for an adaptation of Sophocles' *Antigone*.
	12 December, completion of *Antigone*.
1948	15 February, first performance of the *Antigone* adaptation in Chur.
	5 June, first performance of *Herr Puntila und sein Knecht Matti* in Zurich.
	July, working on the *Kleines Organon für das Theater*, a project he had first begun in 1946.
	18 July, the *Kleines Organon* 'more or less finished'.
	20 September, preparations for a trip to Berlin where he is to stage a production of *Mutter Courage*.
	20 October, since Brecht is refused a visa by the American authorities, he travels to Berlin via Prague.
1949	11 January, Berlin première of *Mutter Courage*.
	4 March, discussions with Caspar Neher in Zurich on the possibility of adapting Nordahl Grieg's play about the Paris Commune.
	21 April, a provisional version of *Die Tage der Commune* is ready.
	December, because a production of *Die Tage der Commune* has to be postponed, Brecht turns to Lenz's *Der Hofmeister* which he adapts for performance by the Berliner Ensemble. The same year sees a number of Brecht's works published for the first time.
1950	15 April, première of *Der Hofmeister*.
	14 September, Brecht informs the composer Gottfried von Einem, whom he had approached for assistance in

April 1949, that he has received approval of his application for Austrian citizenship.

1951 15 January, discussions with Paul Dessau concerning the forthcoming production of 'Das Verhör des Lukullus'. They encounter difficulties with the party officials: in March, after the first performance, the title is altered to *Die Verurteilung des Lukullus*.

24 March, première of Brecht's adaptation of Gerhart Hauptmann's *Der Biberpelz* and *Roter Hahn*.

May, Brecht considering an adaptation of Shakespeare's *Coriolanus*.

29 June, Emil Burri, together with Brecht, has written a film-script of *Mutter Courage*.

3 October, discussions with D.E.F.A. concerning the projected film: alterations to the script are suggested by Brecht and Burri.

12 October, first performance of the opera *Die Verurteilung des Lukullus* in Berlin.

Publication of the volume *Hundert Gedichte*, a selection of Brecht's verse made in collaboration with Wieland Herzfelde.

1952 23 April, première of Brecht's reworking of Goethe's *Urfaust*.

August, working with Hanns Eisler on the libretto for the latter's project *Doktor Faustus*.

December, further work on the *Coriolanus* project, which he had been revising during the year.

1953 17 January, Brecht informs Emil Burri that the controversy and arguments with D.E.F.A. about the *Courage* film have left him despondent and he has lost all interest in the film's progress.

17 June, the uprising in East Berlin.

During the Summer, Brecht spends most of the time in his house in Buckow, where he writes poems and works on the drama *Turandot oder Der Kongress der Weisswäscher*.

1954 19 March, the Berliner Ensemble moves into its own theatre, the Theater am Schiffbauerdamm. The opening production is Brecht's adaptation of Molière's *Don Juan*.

In the early part of the year, Brecht conducts rehearsals for *Turandot*, but his principal concern is with a production of *Der kaukasische Kreidekreis*.

7 October, première of *Der kaukasische Kreidekreis*.

21 December, Brecht awarded the Stalin Peace Prize.

1955   March/April, adaptation of Farquhar's *The Recruiting Officer*.

28 June, Brecht, Burri and Wolfgang Staudte complete a final draft of the film-script for *Mutter Courage*.

18 August, shooting begins, but after Brecht's continuing objections, is broken off.

19 September, première of the Farquhar adaptation, re-titled *Pauken und Trompeten*.

Mid-December, begins the rehearsals for a production of *Leben des Galilei*.

1956   Rehearsals for the production continue: in May Brecht is hospitalized, suffering from the after-effects of virus flu. In June and July he spends most of the time in Buckow: his health is poor.

10 August, attends rehearsals of *Leben des Galilei* for the last time.

14 August, death of Brecht.

17 August, burial in the Dorotheen-Friedhof in East Berlin.

Select Bibliography

1. PRIMARY LITERATURE: *German editions:*
   Bertolt Brecht *Gesammelte Werke 1–20* (*GW*), Frankfurt am Main, 1967; *Über Lyrik* (*ÜL*), Frankfurt, 1968 (3rd edition); *Arbeitsjournal 1938–55* (*AJ*), Frankfurt, 1973; *Schriften zum Theater* (*SzT*), Frankfurt, 1963.
   English edition: John Willett & Ralph Mannheim (eds): *Collected Works of Bertolt Brecht*, (in progress), London and New York.

2. SECONDARY LITERATURE
   Anon 'Brecht in Exile', in *T.L.S.*, 23 November 1973.
   Hannah Arendt 'Profiles. What is permitted to Jove', in *The New Yorker* (*NY*), 5 November 1966.
   Eric Bentley (ed) *Thirty Years of Treason*, London, 1972.
   Eric Bentley 'The Science Fiction of Bertolt Brecht', in *Evergreen Review 10*, (1966), pp. 29ff.
   Thomas K. Brown 'Brecht and the 17th of June 1953', in *Monatshefte 63*, 1971, pp. 48–55.
   Hans Bunge *Fragen Sie mehr über Brecht*, Munich, 1970.
   Peter Demetz (ed) *Brecht—A collection of critical essays*, New Jersey, 1962.
   Alfred Döblin *Aufsätze zur Literatur*, Freiburg, 1963.
   Martin Esslin *Brecht, a Choice of Evils*, London, 1959.
   Max Frisch *Tagebuch 1946–1949* (*T1*), Knaur Taschenbuch, Munich/Zurich, 1967.
   Max Frisch *Tagebuch 1966–1971* (*T2*), Frankfurt, 1972.
   Graham Greene *The Pleasure Dome*, London, 1972.
   Matthew Hodgart *Satire*, World University Library 43, London, 1969.
   Hans Otto Münsterer *Bert Brecht. Erinnerungen aus den Jahren 1917–1922*, Zurich, 1963.
   Dieter Schmidt *Baal und der junge Brecht*, Stuttgart, 1966.
   Walter Theimer *Der Marxismus*, Bern/Munich, 1969 5th edition.

Klaus Völker *Brecht-Chronik*, Munich, 1971.

John Willett *The Theatre of Bertolt Brecht*, London, 1967 3rd edition—first published 1959.

3. SUGGESTIONS FOR FURTHER READING

Heinz Ludwig Arnold (ed) Bertolt Brecht I and II. Sonderbände aus der Reihe *Text und Kritik*, Munich, 1972 and 1973.

Gisela Bahr, John Fuegi, Reinhold Grimm (eds) *Brecht Heute 1, 2, 3*, Frankfurt.

Gisela Bahr, John Fuegi, Reinhold Grimm *Brecht Jahrbuch 1974*, Frankfurt.

Walter Benjamin *Versuche über Brecht* Frankfurt, 1966. English edition (translated by Anna Bostock and with introduction by Stanley Mitchell) *Understanding Brecht*, London, 1973.

Werner Frisch and K. W. Obermeier *Brecht in Augsburg*, Frankfurt, 1976.

Reinhold Grimm *Bertolt Brecht*, Stuttgart, 1971. 3rd edition.

James K. Lyon *Bertolt Brecht and Rudyard Kipling*, The Hague, 1975.

James K. Lyon 'Bertolt Brecht's Hollywood Years: the dramatist as film writer' in *Oxford German Studies 6*, 1971–2, pp. 145–74.

Hans Mayer *Brecht in der Geschichte*, Frankfurt, 1971.

Siegfried Mews and Herbert Knust (eds) *Essays on Brecht*, University of North Carolina Press, 1974.

Michael Morley ' "Progress is the Law of Life": Brecht's poem *Die Internationale*', in *German Life and Letters* April 1970, pp. 255–68; ' "The Light that Shineth More and More": Another Look at Kipling's Influence on Brecht', in *Modern Language Notes 88*, April 1973, pp. 562–73.

Manfred Riedel 'Bertolt Brecht und die Philosophie' in *Neuer Rundschau 82*, 1971, pp. 145–54.

Klaus Schuhmann *Der Lyriker Bertolt Brecht 1913–1933*, dtv, Munich, 1971.

Anthony Tatlow *Brechts chinesische Gedichte*, Frankfurt, 1973.